WOMEN'S DEVELOPMENT AMID CONFLICTS IN KASHMIR

WOMEN'S DEVELOPMENT AMID CONFLICTS IN KASHMIR

A SOCIO-CULTURAL STUDY

Shazia Malik

PARTRIDGE

A Penguin Random House Company

To order additional copies of this book, contact
Partridge India
000 800 10062 62
orders.india@partridgepublishing.com

www.partridgepublishing.com/india

Dedicated to my beautiful daughter Fatima

CONTENTS

ACKNOWLEDGEMENT

At the very outset, I wish to express my deep sense of gratitude to my Supervisor, Dr. Zainudin, for his kind encouragement and support. He took keen interest in my work all along and his critical and insightful comments have been considerably helpful in improving the quality of this work.

I am deeply indebted to my Co-Supervisor, Prof. Farhat Hasan, Department of History, University of Delhi. Without his guidance, this work would not have been possible. He has been a unique combination of mentor, critic, staunch supporter, and tutor. My words fail to acknowledge the kind of help I received from him.

I am also indebted to Professor Shireen Moosvi (Ex-Director Centre for Women's Studies) for her constant encouragement and support. Owing to her efforts, we were provided with a comfortable and helpful environment at the centre, and she took an extraordinary interest in meeting our library and computer-aided requirements.

I am honoured to put on record my special thanks to Professor Emeritus Irfan Habib for the interest and concern he has consistently shown in my research. His suggestions have been great help in improving the quality of this work.

The Centre for Women's Studies (A.M.U, Aligarh) and the faculty and staff associated with it have been a source of considerable encouragement. For lack of space, I cannot mention all of them here but, the following deserve special thanks: Dr. Nadeem Rizvi, Professor Imtiyaz Hasnain, Dr.Ishrat Alam, Dr Shadab Bano and Dr.Ehtisham-ud-din.

During the course of my Research, I had discussions with several eminent scholars of women's studies. I would in particular like to thank, Dr. Mary E.Johns, Dr. Seema Kazi, Dr. Indu Agnihotri and Dr. Vasanthi Raman for their constructive suggestions concerning my work. Dr. B.A.Dabla, who is an authority on Kashmir, was kind enough to discuss my work with me, and his critical observations have certainly saved me from several glaring omissions and inadequacies. I am indebted to a well-known lawyer in Kashmir, Mr.Zafar Shah, for enlightening me about the legal niceties and procedure.

I am grateful to the staff of the following libraries which I visited for collection of research material: Maulana Azad Library(Aligarh Muslim University), National Archives of India (New Delhi), Centre for Women's Development studies (New Delhi), Nehru Memorial museum and Library (New Delhi), Jammu and Kashmir State archives (J&K), Alama Iqbal library (University of Kashmir) Srinagar, Secretariat Library Srinagar, and Doru Shahabad Tehsil Court, Anantnag. I am also thankful to Jammu and Kashmir Coalition of civil society, specially Khurram Parvez and Mohammed Altaf Khan of Jammu and Kashmir Liberation Front. This work would not have been possible without the help of journalist/human rights activist friends namely Mr.Ishfaq Mir (Rising Kashmir), Mr Khalid Gull (Greater Kashmir) and Mr. Rayees, who provided inputs that were so very valuable for my research. Of course, without the co-operation of my respondents, this study, would have never been completed. I am indebted to all my respondents who were very generous to me and shared their innermost feelings with me.

I am grateful to the staff of the Centre for providing library, Xerox and Computer facilities, in particular Mr.Sajid, Mr.Asher, Mr.Waseem, Mr.Sabir, Ms Nighat, Ms Seema and Mr.Amit. I also express my thanks to the faculty at the Centre, Mr.Aziz Faisal, Dr.Huma, Dr.Juhi and Ms.Tauseef for their ungrudging support and encouragement.

My family has been my main source of inspiration I am indebted to all members of my family, especially my Dad, Mr. Gh.Mohi-ud-din Malik whose undaunted support have made me survive difficult times during my research.

Bashir Ahmad Chepoo and Mrs. Safia have shaped my conviction in great many ways. My childhood teacher and uncle, Late Mr. Ishaq had taught me the values of honesty which I tried to hold on with, all through my work. I appreciate my husband Mr. Feroz Ahmad's belief in me and the way he provided moral support to me. Love of my niece Sarah soothed me in difficult times.

SHAZIA

ABBREVIATIONS

AFKP	Association of Kashmiri Prisoners, (Jammu and Kashmir)
AFSPA	Armed Forces Special Power Act 1990
APDP	Association of Parents of Disappeared Persons (Jammu and Kashmir)
BPL	Below Poverty Line
CID	Criminal Investigation Department (India)
CRPF	Central Reserved Police Force (India)
DeM	*Dukhtarane-Millat* (Jammu and Kashmir)
HELP	*Human Efforts for Love and Peace* (Jammu and Kashmir)
HM	*Hizbul Mujahidin*
IWIJ	Independent Women's Initiative for Justice (A fact finding Team who did a Case Watch on Shopian rape/Murder Case)2010
JKCCS	Jammu and Kashmir Coalition of Civil Societies (Jammu and Kashmir)
JKLF	Jammu and Kashmir Liberation Front (Jammu and Kashmir)
KGBV	Kasturba Gandhi Balika Vidhyalaya (India)
KWIPD	Kashmiri Women's Initiative for Peace and Disarmament (Jammu and Kashmir)
MCS	Model Cluster Schools
MKM	*Muslim Khwateen-e-Markaz* (Jammu and Kashmir)

MMR	Maternal Mortality Rate
NAI	National Archives of India, New Delhi
NC	National Conference, Jammu and Kashmir
NFHS	National Family Health Survey(India)
NGO	Non-Governmental Organisation
NPEGEL	National Programmes for Education of Girls and Primary Level (India)
NPP	National Panthers Party (Jammu and Kashmir)
PITA	Prevention of Immoral Trafficking Act, 1956
POTA	Prevention of Terrorism Act 2002
PSA	Public Safety Act, 1978
SF	Security Forces
SHRC	State Human Rights Commission (Jammu and Kashmir)
TADA	Terrorism and Disruptive Activities(Prevention Act), 1987
WSDC	Women's Self Defence Corps (Jammu &Kashmir)
APHC	All Party Hurriyat Conference (Jammu and Kashmir)
WISCOMP	Women's In Security, Conflict Management and Peace (New Delhi)

GRAPHS

TABLES

LIST OF APPENDICES

Number of Appendices

Glossary

Jagir	A Persian word meaning 'place holding'. In Kashmir, Jagir was a type of feudal land grant bestowed by a monarch to a feudal superior in recognition of his administrative and/or military service.
Raja	A Small ruler
Begar	enforced unpaid labour
Mader-e-Maherban	The Kind Mother, in Kashmir two lady's were revered with this name, one was the Wife of Sheikh-Imamu-ud-din of Srinagar and the second was Begum Abdullah.
Kare-sarkar	The work of Government
Allahu-Akbar	Allah is Great
Jai Dev Maharaj	Glory to the King
Ladi Shah	One who recites popular ballads to street crowds
Kangri	Fire-pot, a kind of pot made of clay, filled with burning charcoal, used to warm ones body.
Bhangi	scavengers
Hanji	Fisherman
Dholak	Drum
Hash	Mother-in-law
Nosh	Sister-in-law
Zaam	Husband's Sister
Baikakiney	Brothers wife

Watals	Scheduled castes
Taranga	Traditional Pundit Women's head gear
Qasaba	Ornate head gear worn by traditional Kashmiri Women
Manzim Yor	Go-between, one who arranges marriages
Nabad Nishain	Betrothal, engagement ceremony
Nikah Nishain	Kind of betrothal in which Nikah is also ceremonised
Azadi	Freedom
Phiran	A long loose garment worn by men and women of Kashmir

INTRODUCTION

The growth of feminist scholarship has led to several detailed and well-researched studies on the position of women in India. Feminist scholars have unravelled the social, cultural and economic basis of women's subordinate position in various regions of the Indian subcontinent. Unfortunately, the region of Kashmir has not received the attention it deserves, and the preoccupation with the insurgency in the state has peripheralized issues concerning women and gender relations. The chief objective of my proposed theme of research is to fulfil the lacunae and construct a picture of changing position of women and gender relations in the region of Kashmir, since 1947. It is, of course, well-known that the region is disrupted by continuing cycles of violence, but in the shaping of women's lives and experience; violence is only one, if indeed a dominant, factor. Despite violence, women have developed social ties and affect social capital that have transcended its constraints and restrictions. At the same time, in studying the lives of women in Kashmir, the role of violence cannot be ignored either, and one of the concerns of my study is to examine the effects of the 'culture' of 'violence' on women's development in the region.

My study broadly looks into five major issues; they are;

1. To compare the position of women under the Dogra rule with their position in Post-independence period.
2. To examine the issue of women's development since post-independence period, considering that there has been scarcely any work done on the issue.
3. To study changes in the position of the women since the resurgence of the militancy after 1980's.
4. To examine the impact of violence on the lives of women.
5. To examine the role of the State in women's development.
6. To examine the role of the women's movement in Kashmir.

Literature Review:

Kashmir is indeed a neglected region, and if it has suffered from the neglect of politicians, it has also suffered from the neglect of scholars. Compared to the kind of sophisticated studies on the position of women and gender that we have for the other regions of India, the works on Kashmir are few and far between. One scholar who has extensively worked on women in Kashmir, within a sociological framework, is Bashir Ahmed Dabla. He has written several books on women in Kashmir, but the more important ones are: *Gender discrimination in the Valley*[1], *multidimensional*

---

[1] Dabla Bashir Ahmad, Sandeep.K.Nayak, Khurshid-Ul-Islam(ed.), *Gender Discrimination In the Kashmir Valley; a*

problems of women in Kashmir[2], *Domestic Violence Against Women In Kashmir Valley*[3], *Widows and Orphans In Kashmir*[4], *Sociological Papers on Kashmir Vol. 1 & 2*[5]. A sociologist, Dabla primarily relies on field work for the collection of data, and since no other scholar has made such an effort, his work remains an pioneering one. His study reveals the existence of discrimination against women in education, availability of jobs, nutrition, health etc. All his studies are based on empirical investigation and detailed sample surveys. The data collected by Dabla on the organization of family in Kashmir reveals the deeply structured presence of domestic violence and wife-beating in Kashmir. While one would want to compare the incidence of domestic violence in Kashmir with other Indian states, his findings suggest that it was still relatively lower than the Indian average. Dabla's works are incredibly useful for the present study also because they cover a wide range of issues and through empirical data's his work has credited the other data generated by non-governmental organizations. His works give insights, to issues of gender conflated with militancy, modernization, culture and the politics and becomes an important starting point for carrying forward the further research. There are, however, two difficulties with Dabla's method. For one, his samples

---

survey of Budgam and Baramulla Districts, Gyan Publications, Delhi, 2000

2   Dabla Bashir Ahmad, *Multidmensional Problems of Women In Kashmir,* Gyan Publishing House, Delhi, 2007

3   Dabla, Bashir Ahmad, *Domestic Violence Against Women In Kashmir Valley,* JAYKAY Publications, Srinagar,2009

4   Dabla, Bashir Ahmad, *A Sociological Study of Widows and Orphans in Kashmir,* JAYKAY Publications, Srinagar, 2010

5   Dabla Bashir Ahmad, *Sociological Papers on Kashmir, Volume 1 and 2,* JAYKAY publications, Srinagar, 2010

are extremely modest. His research is narrowly empiricist, and fails to develop theoretical insights from the raw data collected by him. His work *Multidimensional problem of women in Kashmir* dealt with the questions over social (such as dowry), economic, educational, health and discrimination problems. His study suggests discrimination working at various levels such as work places and there is lesser authority than men in day to day life. One of his recent works *Domestic Violence Against Women in Kashmir Valley*, Dabla has attempted to identify major acts of violence against women in the Kashmir Valley in the domestic framework; and the extent to which they are experienced. The empirical data, based on 200 women respondents from all the districts of Kashmir, covers post-marital situations like the separation of a wife from husband and the consequent sufferings for women. Issues of wife-beating, torture/Harrassment, Dowry, Divorce (threats) have also been studied with the support of relevant empirical data. The study reveals that the practice of wife-beating was not carried out by husbands only. In many cases it was done by the members of in-laws family too, and also the practice was carried out by both men and women.

Aneesa Shafi's work on *Working Women in Kashmir*[6] deals with the problems and prospects of employment of women in Kashmir. One of her important findings is that women are attracted to specific professions, in particular, school and college teaching. The title is misleading, for even though the book purports to be about 'working women', it is very vague about what she means by a working woman. She is actually only concerned with women serving in the service sector, and

---

[6]   Aneesa Shafi, *Working Women In Kashmir, Problems and Prospects,* APH publications, Delhi,2002

ignore from her study the waged women workers and women in the unorganized economy.

In *Women, War and Peace in South Asia*[7], a pioneering work in the field, Rita Manchanda examines Kashmiri women's different experiences of conflict. The article titled *Guns and Burqa-Women in the Kashmir conflict*, shifts the focus away from the victimhood discourse (such as The Grieving Mother) and explores women's agency for both peace and conflict. The book explores the ways in which women negotiate violent politics in their everyday lives. Manchanda maps the women in the Kashmir conflict in two narratives. The first derives from a Human Rights discourse where women figure as victims of Direct (state) and indirect violence that transforms them into widows and Half-widows of disappeared or bereaved mothers of lost sons and children. The second centres on the conventional patriarchal ideology of the Kashmiri struggle in which women symbolise the grieving mother, the Martyr's mother and the Raped woman. As she points out, women have innovated forms of resistance grounded in the cultural space of women, especially around mourning for example Association of Parents of Disappeared Persons (APDP), which politicises traditional 'motherist' role by taking the private act of mourning into public space. Women's ways of acting are increasingly challenging the notion of what political activity can be. Manchanda argues that while the dominant militant discourse is organised to direct community/individuals to violence, women have a more ambivalent and shifting understanding of

---

[7]   Manchanda Rita(ed.), *Women, War and Peace in South Asia; Beyond Victimhood to Agency*, Sage Publications, New Delhi,2001

the legitimacy or illegitimacy of violence according to the evolution of armed struggle.

Urvashi Butalia, in her study, *Speaking Peace: Women's Voices from Kashmir*[8], communicates the voices of all the major communities that constitute the troubled State of Kashmir. Perhaps the first of its kind in Kashmir, it documents the testimonies of ordinary and extraordinary women. It brings forth the complexities of a situation where women of Kashmir become victims of all the 'others'. Batalia has shown in her work how women of Kashmir are targeted by the state agents, militants and also unfortunately by their own community, most of the times for none of their faults. Her works is an important departure for my work as one gets acquainted with the kinds of dilemmas for women and my work strives to find how they cope under such complexities and how dynamic these complexities remain over a period of time? It narrates the perspectives of women in Kashmir who reject the discourses of violence on women through moral policing. And also puts forward the dilemma's of women who conform to these prescribed rules unwillingly.

Between Democracy & Nation; Gender and Militarisation in Kashmir[9] by Seema Kazi, contextualises the past two decades of militarisation in Jammu & Kashmir, exploring the involvement of both Kashmiri militants and Indian military forces. In addition, however, it also critically highlights the conflict but largely overlooked gender dimensions. Based on

---

[8]   Urvashi Batalia(ed.), *Women's Voices from Kashmir*, Kali for Women, New Delhi,2002

[9]   Kazi Seema, *Between Democracy and Nation-Gender and Militarization in Kashmir*, Women Unlimited, New Delhi, 2009

personal narratives of people, Kazi had met and interviewed, the author explores Kashmiri women's political experience of militarisation, demonstrating how the struggle for freedom "centres on women's conventional role as mothers, wives and sisters". While Kashmiri women actively participated in the movement for Azadi through public protests and as couriers, supporters and nurses, while also providing other logistical and moral backup, there have been no women in the decision-making bodies of the separatist parties to date.

In *Women Islam and violence in Kashmir*[10], Nyla Ali Khan, investigates the effects of nationalist, militant, and religious discourses and praxes on a gender-based hierarchy. The book analyzes the development of the Kashmiri crisis through literature, history, and ethnography while foregrounding the status of women.

My effort here is to explore the impact of violence on women's development, and the complex entanglement of the culture of violence with the disempowerment of women. Under this broad theme, my study makes an attempt to make a qualitative estimate of the scale of violence in Kashmir, and the extent to which violence constrains women, and prevents their development in the region. The study attempts to uncover women's voices that have experienced violence, and to develop a framework to analyse the culture of violence within a gendered, sociological framework. It has been argued by historians working on partition violence, that violence against women is always met with silence. Women who are victims of violence are

---

[10]   Khan Nyla Ali, *Islam, Women and Violence in Kahsmir; Between India and Pakistan,* Palgrave Macmillan, New York, 2010

never allowed to express their grief and suffering, and one of the efforts of my study is to lend a voice to their silence, to provide, as it were, spaces for the articulation of their experiences and agency.

Method:

The present study is a sociological and a feminist study, which has been carried out by combination of both qualitative as well as quantitative approaches. In my filed survey I have followed the methodology of field work laid down by Aan Oaklay who argues that there is a feminist way of conducting interviews which is superior to a more dominant masculine model of such research[11]. Oaklay points out; 'feminist methodology requires further, that the methodology of 'hygiene' research with its accompanying mystification of the researcher and the researched as objective instincts of data production be replaced by the recognition that personal involvement is more than dangerous bais—it is the condition under which people come to know each other and to admit others into their lives'.

Confirming to the method prescribed for a feminist Researcher, I have kept in view the Standpoint epistemology, and refused to see the 'facts' or 'data' as separated from the realm of experience[12]. Standpoint epistemology being an

---

[11] Oakley.A, Interviewing Women: Contradiction in Terms, IN Roberts, H. (ed.). *Doing Feminist Research*, Routledge & Kegan Paul, London 1981, p- 30-61.

[12] See Maithre Wickramasinghe, *Feminist Research Methodology- Making Meanings of Meaning Making*, Routledge, USA, 2010, p- 55-71

innovative approach of knowledge building breaks down boundaries between academia and activism, between theory and practice[13]. This approach has been followed throughout the work. Feminist Standpoint Scholars such as Abigail Brooks, argue that women, as members of an oppressed group, have cultivated a double consciousness—a heightened awareness not only of their own lives but of the lives of the dominant group (men) as well[14]. She has further argued that Women are tuned in to men's activities, attitudes and behaviours and to their own[15].

This approach, as viewed by Abigail Brooks, not only takes women seriously as knowers but also attempts to translate women's knowledge into practice, so that apply what is learned from women's experience be applied towards social change and towards the elimination of the oppression not only of women but of all marginalized[16].

Indeed, in collecting information, it was assumed that there is no single/unilateral version of truth, and our subjective experiences and social locations determine our perception of truth or falsehood. At the same time, it is understood that certain experiences of women are gender specific; emerging from their exclusions they suffer by virtue of their sex.

---

[13] Abigail Brooks, 'Feminist Standpoint Epistemology: Building Knowledge and Empowerment Through Women's Lived Experience', IN Sharlene Nagy Hesse-Biber, Patricia Lina Leavy(ed.), *Feminist Research Practice*, Sage Publications, London, New Delhi, 2007, p-77

[14] Ibid p-63

[15] Ibid p-66

[16] Ibid p-76

Nature of Data/Sources:

The unit of analysis for my research was the Kashmiri society inhabited in the Kashmir province in Jammu And Kashmir State. I have selected two districts in Kashmir for a focused study-Anantnag in South Kashmir and Srinagar in North Kashmir. Anantnag District is in the southern sector of Jhelum Valley. The area under the district after carving out Kulgam in 2007 stood at 2917 sq.km and constitutes 1.31% of the total area of Jammu and Kashmir State. As per 2001 census, the population of the districts is 7.34 lacs with 3.85lacs males and 3.49lacs females[17]. The distribution of population between rural and urban stands in the ration of 80:20. The district consists of 393 villages, 01Muncipal Council and 10 Municpal committees. There are six Tehsils, viz; Anantnag, Bijbehara, Dooru, Shangus, Kokernag and Pahalgam[18]. Srinagar district is situated in the centre of Kashmir Valley. As per 2001 census the district has a population of around 10.94 lacs with 6.4 lacs males and 5.5 lacs females[19]. Srinagar district is spread over an area of 294sq.Km[20]. This study was carried out through interview Schedules, supplemented by official/unofficial data, archival records and also secondary works done in the relevant field. A detailed interview schedule composing 22 set of questions was framed (Appendix A). Since my respondents included

---

[17]   Census of India, J&K, 2001, Government of India, *www. censusofIndia.com*

[18]   *http://anantnag.nic.in/* official website of District Anantnag, Government of J&K

[19]   Census of India, J&K, 2001, Government of India, *www. censusofindia.com*

[20]   *http://Srinagar.nic.in/districtprofile/districtprofile.htm* official website of District Srinagar, Government of J&K

illiterate persons, as well, their responses were communicated to me orally, and were then entered by me in the data sheet. The total number of respondents was 200 selected on the basis of the total number of population of women in the Valley. The sampling was done randomly and constituted only women respondents. Respondents were categorized on the basis of

I) Income[21]:

    a)   Upper class (60 Respondents)

    b)   Middle class (80 Respondents)

    c)   Lower class (60 Respondents)

II) Residence:

    a)   Rural and b) urban.

As against a synchronic study, my work adopts a diachronic framework, and studies issues of women's development in the context of changing political, social and economic developments. In other words, issues in women's development are examined in their changing socio-economic and political contexts.

Over-view of Chapters:

While I do not wish to make comparisons with other Indian states here, my research would, hopefully, allow for such a comparative study, and enable interested researchers in

---

[21]   Annual Family Income; Upper Class: 5,00000-10,00000 and Above, Middle Class: 1,50000 to 5,00000, Lower Class: Below 1,50000

comparing the position of women in Kashmir with their position in other states of India.

The present study contains four chapters. Chapter I is entitled, 'Women in Kashmir; A Historical Background'. I have attempted to examine the position of women under the Dogra rule. I have studied the position of women in general and the marginalized women in particular focusing all along the nature of their relations with the state. I have delineated the state's alliance with the patriarchy though archival reports and other historical documents. One of the issues that I highlight is the appropriation of women's bodies by the state. I have also looked at the nature of the participation of Kashmiri women in the struggle for independence against Dogra rule.

Chapter II, entitled 'Women in the family and community life' attempts to examine the issue of women's development in the post-independent period. I have charted the Women's development in Kashmir along the following main indices: family, education, property and health.

To study the matter I have made an effort to look at the lives and experiences of women in their families and community units. While the chapter is mainly based on my field work, I have tried to apply theoretical perspectives based on my understanding of the certain selected studies in the analysis of the data.

The chapter entitled, 'Women and the armed conflict in Kashmir' deals with the effects of insurgency on the lives of women in Kashmir. The chapter attempts to explore women's agency in Kashmir when faced with regular, routine violence. In ethnic conflict, women are treated as markers of community identity, and are targeted to humiliate the community. The patriarchal forces within the community are no less severe on their own women, and control and discipline them in the name of the honor of the community. In Kashmir, one of the important consequences of the long decades of violence has been the emergence of female headed households. I also examine the nature of these households, in particular, their organization, distribution of affect and power. Violence, death and disappearances abruptly thrust upon these women positions of responsibility, forcing them to reorganise the household destroyed by the death of the bread earner. I have attempted to examine the consequence of the violence on the bodies of women during the conflict era in Kashmir, which still remains unabated. While one looks upon the violence as male dominated and male oriented, it becomes significant to study the social effects of such dreadful violence on women's lives so as to see how women situate themselves when their male breadwinners die or disappear. I have also looked into the issues of women as cultural markers of their community identity, which makes them vulnerable to various kinds of policing. Further I have tried to see how women in Kashmir retained the fabric of the family and community despite repeated violence, deaths and encounters.

In Chapter four my purpose has been mainly to find out the motives behind women's organization's support to the ideologies of militant organizations. Here, I have noticed that women's movements have had 'complex and contradictory' roles to play in Kashmir. While there have been women's political organizations that have, supported militant organizations, there have been several others who have courageously confronted them, as well. Looking at the activities of women's movements in Kashmir, one is visibly struck by the level of their political consciousness, and wide social support.

APPENDIX-A

Interview Schedule

Date: _____

Place: _____

Name of the respondent: _____ (optional)

Religion:_____

Age: _____

Status:
  a) Earning
  b) Non-earning

If your answer to the above question is (a), Specify your means of earning
  a) Full time employment
  b) Seasonal / part time employment
  c) Domestic handicraft employment
  d) Any other (specify)

Family income (annual):
  a) 10, 00000 and above
  b) 500000-100000
  c) 150000-500000
  d) Less than 150000

Place of residence: Rural/urban

Size of the family:
  a) total members:
  b) no. of children: Boys _____Girls_____
  c) Other members (specify):

Nature of Family: Joint Family / Nuclear family

1. Do you take help of a maid in your household chores?
    Specify the type of labor.
    a) Always
    b) Never
    c) Sometimes

    _____
    _____

2. Does your spouse help you in your domestic chores?
    Specify the frequency and the type of work?

    _____
    _____
    _____

3. As a woman, were you discriminated against in matters of:
    a) Education   Yes/No
    b) Health   Yes/No
    c) Choice of Career   Yes/No
    d) Sports and Outdoor activities   Yes/No
    e) Food and nutrition   Yes/No
    f) Love and affection   Yes/No

4. How often do you take part in the discussions in the family concerning property, finance and the future of the children?
   a) Never
   b) Frequently
   c) Sometimes

5. Does your spouse beat you
   a) Never
   b) Frequently
   c) Sometimes
   d) In the past (but not in the present)

6. Does your family restrict your movement
   a) Never
   b) Very often
   c) occasionally
   d) always

7. You see your spouse as a:
   a) friend
   b) partner
   c) master
   d) guardian

8. Do female members in your natal family have a share in property? YES/NO

9. Did you inherit property from your parents?   YES/NO
   If your answer to the above question is positive, then what is the proportion of your share to inherited property? _____

_____

10. Which profession does your family favour for your daughters?
    a) Teaching
    b) Medical doctor
    c) Lawyer
    d) Any profession
    e) Nurses
    f) none

11. Did your spouse and/or in laws torture you for not bringing a handsome dowry?
    a) physically
    b) emotionally
    c) both
    d) none

12. Have your husband or in laws derided you for giving birth to a female child?   YES/NO

13. Specify your kind of marriage:
    a) Arranged
    b) Self selection approved by family
    c) Self selection without the approval of your family
    d) Forcible

14. Do you observe *purdah*:
    a) Yes
    b) No

15. If your answer to the above question is (a), what is your perception of *purdah*:
    a) Covering of head (with *dupattai*)
    b) Veiling of face (*burqa*)
    c) Covering the body with a sheet (*chadar*)

16. Did you observe *Purdah* before marriage?
    a) Always
    b) sometimes
    c) never

17. What has been the impact of the militant dicktats on *purdah*?
    a) *Purdah* has become almost mandatory, and more and more women are forced to practice it.
    b) There has been no impact of the militant orders on purdah
    c) Covering of heads in public spaces has almost become mandatory.

18. Did your spouse instruct you to observe *Purdah*? Yes/No

19. How has the militancy in Kashmir changed the dress of women
    a) Increasingly, women have discarded western dresses. Yes/No
    b) Increasingly, women have discarded *sarees*. Yes/No
    c) Women cannot wear clothes that reveal their bodies. Yes/No
    d) Women are forced to cover their heads and wear *abaya* in public places. Yes/No

20. Have you ever suffered sexual harassment at the hands of armed forces?   Yes/No

21. Did you ever suffer eve teasing by armed forces?   Yes/No

22. Do you know of any instance of sexual harassment by military or militant outfits in your neighborhood?

    _____

    _____

    _____

CHAPTER I

WOMEN IN KASHMIR: A HISTORICAL BACKGROUND

**Women's Resistance Against the
Dogra Rule in Kashmir.**

As is well-known, Kashmir was under the oppressive rule of the Dogras during the colonial period. In the people's struggle against the Dogra rule, it is often not recognized that women played an extremely important role. This chapter highlights the contribution of women in the struggle against the Dogra rule in Kashmir, focusing, in particular, on the period from 1930 to 1947. Indeed, women fought shoulder to shoulder with men, and even took up arms against the Dogra rulers. Women's active participation certainly makes the event a glorious chapter in the long history of popular resistance in Kashmir.

The Jammu and Kashmir State is composed of three main cultural units and geographical divisions: Jammu, Kashmir and Ladakh. The state came into existence as a result of the conquest of the Punjab by the British in 1845[22]. The state with its present boundaries was founded by Maharaja Gulab Singh. In 1820, the Maharaja had obtained the principality of Jammu as a *Jagir* from Maharaja Ranjit Singh of the Punjab in recognition of his loyal services. Ranjit Singh authorized him to rule over Jammu as the Raja of the place[23]. The Anglo-Sikh war was concluded with the treaty of Lahore on 9 March 1846; the treaty recognized the independent sovereignty of Raja Gulab Singh in hills as "may be made over to him by a separate treaty"[24]. It created a new and separate territorial entity—Kashmir out of the Sikh territory which was placed under the sovereign authority of Raja Gulab Singh. A separate agreement was concluded by East India Company with Raja Gulab Singh at Amritsar on 16th March 1846. This agreement is popularly known as the 'treaty of Amritsar'. Under this treaty Kashmir was sold to Gulab Singh in lieu of a cash payment of Rupees seventy five lakhs.[25] The same treaty recognized Gulab Singh as the Maharaja of the J&K state. Under the treaty the British promised aid and assistance to the maharaja for defending and protecting his territories from external enemies.[26]

---

[22] Khan G.H, *Freedom Movement in Kashmir 1931-1940*; Light and Life Publications, New Delhi, Jammu, Trivandrum, 1980, pp.ix

[23] Ibid p. 1

[24] *The treaty of Lahore*, article xii, cited from Khan .G.H. *Freedom Movement in Kashmir*, p.3

[25] *Treaty of Amritsar* article iii cited from Khan.G.H., *Freeedom Movement in Kashmir*, p. 3

[26] Ibid

The innocent people of Kashmir were subjected to double tyranny. Being a protected state under British crown, they were tyrannized by both the British state and the Dogra rulers.

Under the Dogras, the people of Kashmir suffered untold miseries. The peasants suffered from inexorably high taxation, and the cruel and harsh methods of tax collection. The ordinary people were faced with a corrupt administration, looking for pretexts to impoverish them. Debt bondage was rampant, and according to one estimate, about 80% of the rural population was under debt[27]. The merchant-moneylenders made fortunes by usury and rack-renting, and lives for ordinary villagers were utterly miserable. True to its oppressive, feudal character, the state claimed to be the proprietor of all land, and while the producing classes were its tenants, land, and all its produce, belonged to the state.[28]

The most pernicious method of oppression was the system of *begar* or forced labor. The officials enforced *begar* not only to meet their personal gains, but also to secure free labor in agricultural fields[29]. In other words, vast masses of Kashmiri people suffered from servitude during the Dogra regime.

The people of Kashmir launched several important movements of resistance against the oppression of the Dogras, and in all these efforts the presence of women was

---

[27]   Khan.G.H, *Freedom Movemnt in Kashmir,* p. 11

[28]   J&K State Archives, Letter from Maharaja Pratab Singh to his Prime Minister, December 14 1918, file no. 191/h-75, Kashmir Government Records.

[29]   Khan.G.H. *Freedom Movement in Kashmir,* p -13

conspicuous. Perhaps, the first armed engagement occurred in Gilgit when Maharaja Gulab Singh invaded the place. The glorious struggle by the people of Gilgit repulsed the invading Maharaja's forces, and inflicted on them a convincing defeat.

The people of Gilgit, supported by women, provided stiff resistance when Maharaja Gulab Singh launched a military expedition against Gilgit. The Dogra forces were defeated by the valiant heroes of Gilgit under the command of Gowhar Rehman. Similarly the people of Hazara Rampur and the gun makers of Srinagar offered stiff resistance when Gulab Singh sent troops under Wazir Lakhpat to takeover the charge of the Kashmir valley from the then Governor, sheikh Imam-ud-din who had already declared his independence. In the encounter the sheikh defeated the Dogra forces with the popular support. In the victory, an important role was played by the wife of Sheikh Imam-ud-din. (She was "a Women of determined courage and character, revered by her subjects as *Madar-i-Meherban* who took up arms and took the vow not to allow the sheikh enter her chambers until he repulsed the invaders. With the help of British Soldiers the people's resistance was however, crushed as in the case of Gilgit.[30]

It is often not recognized that Kashmir was politically active during the Khilafat movement[31], and the people of Kashmir joined the Khilafat and non-cooperation movement in large numbers. In May 1920, Ghandhiji gave the call for

---

[30]   Ibid p.78

[31]   Foe details see Hasan Mushirul, *Nationalism and Communal Politics in India,1855-1930,* Manohar Publications 1991 and Gail Minault, *The Khilafat Movement : Religious Symbolism and Mobilization in India* Columbia University Press,1982

non—cooperation movement, and the impact of his call was felt in Kashmir, as well. The Kashmir people suffering under the oppressive Dogra rule, identified their immediate oppressors—the Dogra rule, identified their immediate oppressors—the Dogras-With the colonial state, and joined the national movement and strongly supported Gandhiji's cell for non-cooperation against the British rule in India. The movement did not, indeed, last long, but it did, for the first time, enable the Kashmiri people, in particular the Muslims, to identify themselves with the movement for anti-colonial resistance and nationalism[32].

An important event in the freedom struggle in the state was the memorandum presented to the Viceroy and Governor General of India, lord Reading in 1924 by freedom fighters of Kashmir.[33] The Memorandum proved costly and the government took severe action against the authors of the memorandum. Government took severe action against the authors of the memorandum. The leading memorialist Saad-ud-din shawl was banished from the state and one Khwaja Shah Naqashbandi was deprived of his *Jagir*.[34] The impact of the Indian Nationalist movement was strongly felt by the educated youth of the state[35]. The non-cooperation movement and the *Jallianwalla Bagh* tragedy were closely watched by them. Many students from the state participated in the non-cooperation campaigns. By 1930 the influence of the Indian nationalism was quite visible in the Kashmir province. The arrest of Mahatma Gandhi on May 1930 was

[32]   Khan, G.H., *Freedom Movement In Kashmir.*, p.82

[33]   Rashid Tasir, *Tarikh-e-Hurriyat-i-Kashmir*, Srinagar Muhaffiz Publication 1968), p. 71

[34]   Khan, G.H., *Freedom Movement in Kashmir*, p. 95

[35]   ibid p.99

protested by the students in Srinagar[36]. With the advent of the English Resident in Kashmir the Christian missionaries arrived as well.[37] The Christian missionaries established schools in Kashmir, and while they did not succeed in converting the Kashmiri's, they did succeed in spreading modern education among them. The spread of modern education made them even more conscious of the oppressive nature of the Dogra Rule, and the support it received from the colonial state. It also enabled them to acquire more modern and sophisticated methods of organizations, mobilization and resistance.[38]

The year 1931 saw the beginning of an organized freedom struggle initiated by the Kashmiris against the autocratic rule of the Dogras in which they had been suffering untold miseries for more than eight decades. The Muslims in Kashmir played an active role in the struggle against the Dogra rule. There were many causes of Muslim unrest. More than 80% of the Muslim population lived on agriculture, but they enjoyed no propriety rights in land. A peasant in Kashmir could be ejected any time by the state[39]. The institution of *kare-sarkar* was introduced as a substitute for the *begar* which had been abolished in 1920. Under *kare-sarkar* the villagers were required to render services for the state whenever demanded. Further the policy of provincialism and racial discrimination followed by the Dogra rulers was bound to create the atmosphere of apathy

[36]   Ibid p.100

[37]   Mohammed Yasin, Madhavi Yasin(ed.), *Mysteries and Glimpses of Kashmir,* Raj Publications, New Delhi, 1996, p.195-196

[38]   Khan, G.H., *Freedom Movement in Kashmir,* p.101

[39]   Ibid

amongst those against whom such policy was directed.[40] The immediate causes which led to the political disturbances of July 1931 can be attributed to the emergence of a group of educated Muslims with modern outlook. They were deeply concerned with the pathetic condition of the peasants and workers, and the lack of employment opportunities for the educated youths in the state.[41]

Role of women:

The women of Kashmir played a conspicuous role in the struggle against the Dogra rule[42]. In a meeting at *Khanqa-he-Maula*, one Abdul Qadeer, a non-Kashmiri Muslim who was in Srinagar came on the stage and said "we do not have guns, but we have plenty of stones and brickbats."[43] On June 25, 1931 he was arrested. The trial of Abdul Qadeer started on July6, 1931 at session's high court, Srinagar. [44] On July 13, 1931, the judgment was pronounced at the central jail, Srinagar. According to an estimate a mob of 4 to five thousand people had gone to witness the trial. They shouted the slogans *"Allaho-akbar" "Qadeer Zindabaad"* and in a short while the police started firing the protestors, killing a large number among them. Remarkably, the women of the working classes of the Muslim society fought shoulder

---

[40]   Ibid, p. 118

[41]   Ibid, p. 122-123

[42]   Bazaz.P.N., *Daughters of Vitasta* Pamposh Publications New Delhi 1959 reprint, Gulshan Publications Srinagar 2005 p. 246, 261,263.

[43]   Cited from, Khan, G.H., *Freedom Movement in Kashmir*, p.130

[44]   Ibid p.131

to shoulder with their counterpart against the injustice and misrule of the Dogra despots. Clearly, then during its first phase of the freedom struggle, the women participants came from the lower sections of society, illiterate and uneducated. These women of the lower orders were not led and organized by educated women but it was their movement that educated women joined later in the period.[45]

With the imposition of martial law, a reign of terror was let loose in the city of Srinagar. The Kashmiris were forced to kiss the Dogra flag and lick the shoes of the soldiers and salute every soldier with the Dogra salutation, "*Jai Dev Maharaj*". Hand written revolutionary posters appeared in Srinagar after the arrest of Sheikh Mohammed Abdullah. During this period women processionists, many of them with suckling babies in their arms, passed through the streets raising slogans against the oppressive Dogra regime and demanding the release of their imprisoned leaders and for the establishment of a democracy in Kashmir. The protesting women were surrounded by the armed police and were ordered to disperse. On their refusal, they were abused, molested, and then killed in large numbers by the agents of the state. Their bodies were recovered from the river in the Srinagar, where they have been dumped by the police. Women came out in procession on July 27 again, carrying black flags. In 1931 when the government handed over the military administration to the command on September 6, a crowd of women agitators was *Lathi* charged and their modesty outraged; 10 women received injuries. Addressing the procession on 2nd August 1931, a Kashmiri women speaker said;

---

[45] Mohammed Yasin and Madhvi Yasin (ed.), *Mysteries and Glimpses of Kashmir*, p. 197-198

Our men should sit in their homes and wear Burqas! We are proud of our Punjabi Muslim brethren but so far they have confined themselves to merely issuing statements. We request the members of British parliament to take our grievances to the League of Nations. We appeal to the army not to oppress women as it was no chivalry. But if they have any such instructions, they will find us ready to meet the challenge.[46]

In the city the processions of women and children had become a common sight and every minute, news of these processions were coming from different parts of the city[47]. It was a common sight to see a *Ladi shah*[48] performing a ballad against the state, watched, sympathized and encouraged by large groups of women. Most of the ballads had the following refrain line each stanza;

"*kan thaw beh wanai sheri-Kashmir*"

Translation:

Listen I am going to unfurl the story of Sheri-Kashmir. [49]

In response to an appeal issued by the All India Kashmir Committee, Kashmir Day was observed all over the state on 14th August 1931. Its aim was to bring pressure upon the government of India to help the Kashmiris secure

---

[46] Saraf Muhammed Yusuf, *Kashmiris Fight- For Freedom vol.1(1819-1946)*, Ferozons Ltd, Lahore, Pakistan, 1977 p. 382-384

[47] Ibid p.388

[48] one who recites popular ballads to street crowds

[49] Ibid p.393

the basic rights denied to them. A complete *Hartal* was observed and processions were taken out. Meetings were held at *Mazar-e-shohada* which were attended by about thirty thousand women. It was addressed by Sheikh Mohammed Abdullah, Chaudhri Ghulam Abbas Khan and Mistri Yaqub Ali. It was followed by another mass meeting at Jamia Masjid. At the end of the meeting, the blood-stained clothes of the martyrs were displaced to the audience.[50] The Muslims of Delhi celebrated the Kashmir day for two consecutive days[51]. September 24 1931 saw the first armed resistance of the Kashmiri Muslims against the excesses of the government. On September 24 the city of Srinagar was pasted with notices to the effect that the "Mohammedans have no quarrel with the Hindus but have declared Jihad against his highness government[52]." Armed with axes, spades, hoes, scythes, pick-axes, knives, harpoons, swords and sticks, about fifteen thousand people had assembled by 1pm[53].

One of the heroines of 1931 upheaval Fazli died on September 24 1931, when the military opened fire on a procession of women which was parading through the Maisuma bazaar Srinagar. In Shopian, Sajida Bano, aged 25 years, who had recently lost her husband, received a bullet wound in military firing, she was pregnant and died along with the child on the spot.[54] Jan begum, widow of Abel

---

[50] Saraf Muhammed Yusuf, *Kashmiri's Fight for Freedom*, p.397

[51] Khan, G.H, *Freedom Movement in Kashmir*, p.139

[52] Telegram from resident in Kashmir" No. 60-c dated sep 24 931, file no. 423(2) of 1931 home/political secret.

[53] Khan, G.H., *Freedom Movement in Kashmir* p.155

[54] Madhvi Yasin, 'Role of Women in freedom struggle of Kashmir', IN Mohd Yasin and Qayum Yasin(ed.) *History of the*

lone, Srinagar, was killed in a police firing.[55]. These women, illiterate and socially inferior, anticipated the movement led by the educated women in the later phase of the freedom struggle. [56] Another heroine of the upheaval was Jan Ded. Jan Ded was illiterate and came from the lower sections in society and this is why her sacrifice has been ignored in the discourse of the freedom struggle in Kashmir. Her natural talents were not exploited, even though she fought well against the injustices. She was pragmatist and was poles apart from many of the male political leaders of Kashmir in that she advocated secularism and shunned narrow communal loyalties. She was ebullient, outspoken and demanding. She incurred wrath of the top Muslim leaders, and had to retire from the active politics after 1934.[57]

A memorandum was presented to the maharaja, which said:

> *Some constables of the training school who were coming towards the city in a lorry, attacked innocent and peaceful Muslim passersby inflicting death on some and injuries on some others . . . . with promulgation of martial law, army wrought havoc on the Muslim passers—by were murdered; peaceful citizens were forcibly brought out of their homes and tortured and arrested: nothing was left undone to disgrace, dishonor and destroy Muslim homes: women were assaulted*

freedom Struggle in Jammu & Kashmir, light and life Publishers, New Delhi, . 1980 p. 203

[55]   Ibid

[56]   ibid

[57]   ibid

> *and outraged: . . . . wherever it was possible*
> *poor men and women were either drowned or*
> *strangulated*[58].

On 22 September people again collected in the Jamia Masjid and came out in a procession. The army fired several rounds and three protestors were killed on the spot and more than a dozen injured. On the same day the military also opened fire on another procession at Maisuma which included women, killing two men and wounding three, including a woman.[59] Processions of women were a common feature of the agitation in various localities of Srinagar and the towns of Baramulla, Sopore, Islamabad (Anantnag) and Shopian. It goes to the credit of the daughters of the valley that although illiterate and unaware of their rights and traditionally confined to their homes, they braved hardships smilingly and fought shoulder to shoulder with men folk for the emancipation of their country from Dogra rule.[60]

On 18th of August, a Muslim women carrying vegetables for sale was way laid by Pandit boys near *Khankah-e-Sokhta*. Her clothes were torn and she was left almost naked. Soon a dead body of a Muslim Women was recovered from a river she was allegedly drowned by soldiers presumably after rape.[61]

On 28 Jan 1932 a number of women took out a procession. When they reached near the right bank of Jhelum, in the midst of the town, the police blocked their passage and the

---

[58] Saraf Muhammed Yusuf, *Kashmiris Fight For Freedom*-1, p.399
[59] Ibid, p. 403
[60] Ibid, p. 404
[61] Ibid, p. 414

sub-inspector used abusive language against political leaders. Begum Bohru, a widow from Baramulla was carrying a *Kangri* (fire-pot) filled with burning charcoal. She hurled it at the sub-inspector. It crashed straight into his face which was permanently disfigured—the gallant woman was shot dead on the Spot[62].One Noor Gujri, a milkman's daughter, plagued the military and police though her vituperative utterance and pugnacious pranks. She was repeatedly arrested, clamped in prison for a few days and released. The National leaders boosted her and denounced the authorities for imprisoning her[63]. In 1939 the Muslim conference was transformed into National Conference[64]. In 1942 Indian National Congress launched quit India movement, many congress leaders were arrested in connection with the movement. In the middle of 1943 congress leaders were released and these leaders visited Srinagar in the summers of 1944 and 1945. They were in close contact with Sheikh Abdullah. That is why despite sheikh Abdullah's non-participation in the Quit India movement and national conference policy of extending verbal support in war efforts of the allies which ran counter to Congress policy, the far sighted congressman chose to ignore it and made every effort to cement their personal and political bonds with sheikh Abdullah.[65] The annual session of the party was held in Srinagar on the 25th, 29th and 30th September, 1944 in *Pather Masjid*. The session is important in that it adopted a political economic and social Programme for Kashmir known

---

[62] Ibid, p.436-437

[63] Bazaz P.N., *Daughters of Vitasta*, p. 262

[64] Mohammed Yasin and Madhvi Yasin, *Mysteries and Glimpses of Kashmir,* p.18

[65] Saraf Muhammed Yusuf, *Kashmiri's Fight for Freedom*, p.641-642

as "New Kashmir". The historic new Kashmir manifesto granted women the right to vote and contest elections. Women were guaranteed equal rights with men in all fields of national life; political, economic, cultural as also in the state services[66].

Although the freedom movement did not take any agitational shape, in the sense understood by the term between 1939 to May 1944. The movement for reforms and the demand for a responsible government for the setting up of a responsible government continued unabated[67]. Soon after the results of elections in the subcontinent were out the British Government sent a cabinet mission for talks with leaders of political parties for evolving an agreed basis for the transfer of power. Sheikh Abdullah sent them a memorandum known as the Quit Kashmir Memorandum, the Memorandum said;-

> *Today the national demand of the people of Kashmir is not merely the establishment of a system of responsible government, but the right to absolute freedom from autocratic rule of the Dogra . . . , Kashmir is not merely a geographical expression, in the north west of the vast sub-continent of India, famed for its beauty and natural wealth, but it is a land strategically situated, the meeting point of India, China and Russia, and as such has an international significance. Our home land is the cradle of Kashmiri nation which by virtue*

---

[66]   Ibid p.643-644

[67]   Ibid p.663

> *of the homogeneity of its language, culture and*
> *tradition and its common history of suffering,*
> *is today one of the rare places in India where*
> *all communities are backing up a united*
> *national demand.*[68]

Sheikh Abdullah launched the "Quit Kashmir" movement with a highly anti government speech at Srinagar on 15th may 1946[69]. Muslim women not only took out processions in defiance of prohibitory orders but also participated in large numbers in the public meetings held at *Khanqahe-Maula* and Hazratbal. The women of Kashmir from all walks of life came forward with redoubled enthusiasm and energy in support of their beloved leader.[70] One Zoni gujjri was put behind bars as many as nine times. Several times she was attacked by the armed police. She was at that time in her teens, and her husband was dead against her political activities. Wife of a poor working man, politics was no luxury for her; home was to be looked after. Her magnetic oratory drew large throngs of women agitators. Gujri lost her only son aged 12 years when a bullet struck the boy in an assault made by the military police. Another woman, Fatima a Peasant woman was shot dead at Anantnag by the Dogra forces in May 1946, while leading a procession to Voice against the repressive policy of the Maharaja. The Dogra forces had occupied the town and armed soldiers were parading through the streets with pointed bayonets fixed on their guns. Some people took a procession in defiance to the

---

[68] cited from Saraf Muhammed, *Kashmiri's fight for Freedom,* p.669-670

[69] Ibid p.672

[70] Ibid, p. 676

military orders. Fatima, also joined at the head of the women processionists and was attacked by the armed soldiers.[71]

It has often been argued that Sheikh Abdullah launched the "Quit Kashmir Movement" on the advice and inspiration of the congress. This does not, however, seem to be entirely correct, because the official congress newspapers attacked the movement in no uncertain terms. [72] It needs to be admitted still that Jawaharlal Nehru was personally involved on the side of Sheikh Abdulah in the Quit Kashmir Movement.

Begum zainab discarded *purdah* led anti govt. demonstrations and delivered speeches to the NC workers. Collecting donations from charitable sympathizers, she arranged relief for victims of Dogra aggression.[73] Begum Akbar Jahan, wife of Abdullah threw herself in the freedom struggle after sheikh Abdullah and his colleagues were arrested during "Quit Kashmir movement". She led anti-govt. demonstrations and kept the morals of the freedom fighters alive. She not only fought against the Dogra oppression but also collected donations from the people for the victims of the Dogra persecution. In February 1947 the cost of living registered an alarming increase in the state. The national conference set up a food committee with begum Abdullah as chairwomen distributing food on subsidized cost. She started a mass campaign against the rising cost of living.[74]

---

[71] Madhvi Yasin, 'Role of Women in Freedom Struggle in Kashmir' p. 204-206

[72] Ibid, p. 680-81

[73] Bazaz, P.N. *Daughters of Vitasta*, p. 269

[74] Ibid p.687

In 1947, India and Pakistan had come into existence. Sheikh Abdullah was released on September 1947, but he refuse to accept the two nation theory. The decision to accede to either India or Pakistan placed Maharaja Hari Singh in a dilemma. On the one hand, if the State acceded to Pakistan, the maharaja's Dogra Hindu community would find itself in a position of subservience. He nourished hopes of an independent state. In August 1947, Maharaja's regime ratified an agreement with the government of Pakistan. This agreement stipulated that the Pakistan government assume charge of the state's post and telegraph system and supply the state with essential commodities[75], but India refused to sign on it unless the political prisoners were freed. The maharaja refused and the agreement was, thus inconclusive.[76] The National Conference firmly placed its bet on India, and supported the accession of Kashmir to India. [77] The National Conference asked people to collectively donate their weapons and their vehicles. Training session for volunteers were organized. This was the beginning of the people's militia of Kashmir. Girls also joined the militia.[78] Zoni Gujjari, joined women's Defence force and received militia training at a place, where now stands the New Secretariat building. During this period she vigorously struggled to topple the Dogra Regime, and to have a democracy in Kashmir. She was awarded with title *"Zoni Mujahid"* in

[75] Khan Nyla Ali, *Islam, Women and Violence in Kashmir Between India and Pakistan,* Tulika Book, New Delhi, 2009 p.26

[76] Abdullah, Sheikh Muhammed, *Flames of the Chinar: An Autobiography,* tr. by Khushwant Singh, New York, Viking,1993 p. 90

[77] Dasgupta, Jyoti Bhusan, *Jammu and Kashmir,* The Hague: Martinus Nijhoff, 1968 p.95

[78] Abdullah *Flames of Chinar,* p. 94

grateful acknowledgement for her Services[79]. Under the leadership of sheikh Mohammed Abdullah National Militia and women's Defense corps-volunteer forces of men and women were organized to ward off the onslaught by the tribal raiders. With its multifaceted and radical activities, women's self Defence corps (WSDC) was harbinger of social change. Attired in traditional Kashmiri clothes and carrying a gun around her shoulders, zoon Gujjari symbolized the WDSC[80]. Begum Abdullah was also foremost in the women's wing of peace brigade, which fought the Pakistani invaders. Begum Abdullah was a very intelligent woman and devout Muslim.[81] In 1947 when the country was under the grip of communal frenzy, she carried the torch of love and peace to far flung areas of the state. She helped the victims of partition in rehabilitation with a motherly care and love. It was only due to her tireless efforts that the state of Jammu and Kashmir was saved from the communal riots. She was awarded the title of *"Mader-e-Meherban'* (kind mother) by the people of Kashmir[82]. Miss Mehmuda Ahamd Shah, a pioneering educationist and champion of women's empowerment, along with other leader women, was in the forefront of WSDC. During her student days in Lahore she joined the 'Punjab Students federation', which was fighting against the British imperialism. In Kashmir she founded 'Free thinkers society' which gathered under it the intellectuals of the state. Meanwhile she joined the freedom Movement under the leadership of sheikh Abdullah. She

---

[79]   Mohummad Yasin and Madhvi Yasin, *Mysteries and Glimpses of Kashmir,* p.201

[80]   Khan Nyla Ali, *Islam, Women and Violence,* p. 116,

[81]   Saraf Muhammed yusuf, *Kashmiri's Fight for Freedom,* p.495

[82]   Mohammed Yasin and Madhvi Yasin(ed.) *Mysteries and Glimpses of Kashmir,* p. 206

did great service in bringing normalcy to the state, when the sub-continent gripped in communal frenzy. Begum Zainab was a grass root level leader. She fought against the Dogra rule under the auspices of the NC. She took charge of the political dimensions of WSDC and shouldering a gun she was in the forefront, leading women's contingents[83]. Sajida Zameer Ahmad was also associated with the Quit Kashmir Movement in its later stage. She joined the WSDC in 1947 and worked actively in various refugee camps.

To conclude, women in Kashmir played a conspicuous role in the freedom struggle. They left the comfort of their homes and joined the movement for liberation in Kashmir, in large numbers. History has ignored their contribution. One important feature that comes out from my study is that women fought Dogras and the colonial state, alongside men, as their equal partners. Secondly, women's participation was not constrained by class, and women of all classes were seen in the nationalist struggle in Kashmir.

Marginalised Women and the State, in Kashmir: (19th-20th centuries)

Scholars working on Kashmir have largely focused on its political processes, and the nature of its relations with the central government. The recurring and ever increasing cycles of violence and political conflict have actually inhibited scholars from studying the social and cultural developments in the state. There has scarcely been any effort to examine the lives of women, in particular marginalized Women, in the

---

[83]   Ibid 117

state. This work seeks to study the lives of one such group of marginalized women—the prostitutes-in relation to the social and political developments in the state.

In colonial India, Jammu and Kashmir was the only state where prostitution was legalized under law and was not a punishable offense. There could have many reasons for this, and while the role of the culture was certainly important, the pecuniary benefit to state was crucial in its tolerance, even encouragement, under the Dogra rule. The ill-famed trade came to the notice of British Government after the devastated famine in 1877-78. According to the British Official reports, about 15 to 25 percent of the revenues of the state came from taxing the prostitutes, who were for this reason provided licenses by the state. In 1880, there were in Kashmir, according to the Report, 18,715 'registered prostitutes' who gave away a share of their 'income' to the state in the form of taxes. The registered prostitutes, it appears, belonged to the lower sections of society, and a significant number of them actually came from the untouchable classes, such as the *Bhangis* (scavengers) and *Hanjis* (fishermen).[84]

We come to know from the official British records that the prostitutes in Kashmir were usually sold at a tender age by their parents to brothel-keepers for a price that varied from rupees 100 to 200. Child trafficking was officially recognized by the state and the purchase of the girl-child by pimps and brothel-keepers was registered and sealed on stamped paper. The children sold for prostitution were usually cajoled into

---

[84]   National Archives of India, (hereinafter NAI), File no. 86, Foreign Department., Secret-E, March 1883, p.10,

believing that they would be married off. For most poor parents marriage was not an option, for the Dogra state taxed marriages as well, and the tax on marriage was usually so high as to be beyond the reach of the poor parents. Our records inform us that the tax on marriage amounted to as much as Rupees 3 to 8[85].

The prostitutes were divided into three classes according to, what the records term as 'gratification', which, of course, included considerations of the age, income, looks and caste of the prostitutes and were taxed accordingly[86]:

Class-I Prostitute: Rs 40 per annum
Class-II Prostitute: Rs. 20 per annum
Class-III Prostitute: Rs. 10 per annum

The Dogra rule was characterized by an oppressive tax regime, and subjects were taxed under one pretense upon another. Even the dead couldn't be buried save by licensed and privileged grave-diggers. Coolies who were engaged to carry the baggage of travelers surrendered half their earnings to the agents of the state[87]. Under such a coercive regime, the prostitutes could not be spared either. Most parents were driven to selling their daughters under extreme poverty for which, of course, the Dogra regime, and its oppressive tax structure, were crucially responsible[88].

---

[85]   Ibid p.10
[86]   Ibid p.12
[87]   Ibid p.12
[88]   Hassnain, F.M. (ed.), *Kashmir Misgovernment*, Robert Thorp, Gulshan Publications, Srinagar, Kashmir, India,1980

The young girls, once sold for prostitution, had no hopes of release, and were destined to work as 'sex slaves' all their lives. It was of course well-nigh impossible for them to save enough money to buy themselves back, as it were[89]. These unfortunate girls were denied permission to get married and settle down in life. Nor were they allowed to change 'profession', and earn their livelihood through other means[90]. In one instance, a woman who entreated the officers to be allowed to marry and lead a settled life was refused permission to do so. She attempted to fly with a man she wished to marry, but was prevented from doing so and was forced to remain in prostitution[91].

The sale of girls and the traffic in women has been described by Arthur Brinkman, the author of *Wrongs in Kashmir* in the following words:

> '*The classes engaged in it [prostitution] are owned as slaves and others, who were formerly in their position. The authority of the latter is backed by the whole power of the Dogra Maharaja, to whom reverts at their death all the wealth gathered by the prostitutes, during their infamous life. Should one of their bondwomen or dancing girl attempt to leave her degrading profession, she is driven back with the lash and the rod into her mistress's power. These facts are certain*'[92].

---

[89]   Ibid, p. 72
[90]   ibid
[91]   Ibid
[92]   Cited from Ibid, p.71

According to Robert Thorp, there were *nauch* (dancing) girls in the service of the Maharaja. The state charged 103 '*chilkee*' Rupees for giving the license to purchase a dancing girl, and once the girl entered the profession, as it were, she had to shell out money to the state, as well[93].

According to an official British report, the prostitutes were also used as spies by the Dogra rulers. Citing the testimony of one Malik Qutubuddin, the source, tells us that the Maharaja was even using the prostitutes to spy on the English visiting Kashmir. It is said on the authority of Malik kutub-ud-in, that the prostitutes were used as spies on English visitors[94].

The famine of 1877-78 seriously affected the prostitution as well as other trades; and the number of brothels in Kashmir declined to just 30, and the registered prostitutes were reduced to 70 or 80 alone. Accordingly, the tax on the prostitutes was also reduced, as well. In March 1880 it was Rs 2 per woman per Month, or Rs 24 per annum as against Rs 10 to Rs 40 per annum.[95]

The prostitution racket, however, was not just regional, but had by the twentieth century spread to all over India. Kashmiri girls were found in the brothels of other parts of India[96]. According to the census 1921, out of the 2995 prostitutes in the brothels of Bombay, 41 were the natives of Kashmir[97].

---

[93] Ibid, p. 71

[94] NAI, File no.86, Foreign Department., Secret-E, March 1883, p.11

[95] Ibid, p.11

[96] NAI, File no. 469, Home Department, 16 November 1921, p.3,

[97] Ibid p.12

The Rajput landlords, who had been assigned huge *Jagir*s by the Maharaja, informs Thorp, perpetuated the practice of women trafficking. He claims that the Rajput Dogras kept a large number of concubines, some acquired through purchase, others by capture[98]. Thorp is, interestingly corroborated by F.M Hassnain who recounts that during recovery of abducted Muslim girls in the Jammu region during 1947-48, it transpired that these Rajput landlords had kept Hindu girls coming from peasant families as concubines in their households[99].

The contemporary sources bring to light the sad plight of these prostitutes. Sexually transmitted diseases were rampant among them, and there were scarcely any hospitals where they could receive proper treatment. In 1877-79, a total of 12, 977 patients reported for treatment at the Srinagar Mission Hospital. Among them, 2,516 patients were suffering from venereal diseases, most of them prostitutes[100]. The Government of India records report that syphilis and other sexually transmitted diseases were quite widespread among the prostitutes in Kashmir.[101] According to the Henvey's Report, the young English residents were involved in helping prostitution to flourish, and the authorities made no efforts to suppress it, since it was a source of revenues for the state[102]. In an interesting case of the same period, a procuress approached the local court to prevent one of her victims from leaving Kashmir, on the ostensible ground that

---

[98]   Hassnain, F.M.(ed.), *Kashmir Misgovernment*, p.72

[99]   ibid

[100] File no. 86, Foreign department, Secret-E, March 1883, NAI, p.11

[101] ibid

[102] ibid

the girl was in debt, but, as Henvey points out, in reality the owner was merely asserting her right to title to the girl. In a rare departure, the court ruled against the plaintiff, but, Henvey believes, this was owing to the pressure of the British rulers[103].

To legalize the institution of prostitution, the Dogra rulers, sanctioned 'The Public Prostitutes rules 1921', whereby, a prostitute desirous of engaging in prostitution could do so, by registering herself as a 'public prostitute'. The chief clauses of the rules are as follows:-

1. The Rules were applicable to any part of the Jammu and Kashmir if declared applicable thereto by the minister-in-charge of municipalities[104].
2. By "Public Prostitute" was meant any woman who earned her livelihood by offering her person to lewdness for hire[105].
3. Every prostitute starting already in 'business' was required to have her name entered in the register of the place and obtain a certificate of registration[106].
4. Every prostitute was required to make an application in person for registration to the officer charged with preparation of the register.[107]
5. Any registered public prostitute might, at any time apply to have her name removed from the register on

---

[103] Ibid, p.26

[104] Jammu and Kashmir laws, volume 18, *Private Colleges regulation Act 2002 to Regulation Act 1977* JK law Reporter Private Ltd. New Delhi, p.629

[105] ibid

[106] ibid

[107] Ibid, p.630

the ground that she intended to cease the business for which her name was registered and if the officer, in whose register she was entered, was satisfied with her intention, her name would be removed from the register[108].

6. A minister-in-charge of municipalities was empowered to prohibit the keeping of a brothel or the residence of a public prostitute in any specified part of the place to which the rules applied[109].

7. Prostitutes acting in contravention of these rules or any notice or order issued there under would, on conviction before a (judicial magistrate) be liable to be sentenced to a fine not exceeding Rs 100 or simple imprisonment not exceeding a period of one month[110].

Thus, according to public prostitution rules, a prostitute could carry on her trade legally if she registered herself with the district Magistrate. The rules also accepted the role of a brothel keeper and defined him or her as the occupier of any house, room, tent, boat or place resorted to by person of both sexes for the purpose of prostitution. However the brothel keeper had to ensure that he did not keep prostitutes who were not registered with the government[111].

In 1930's a barber of Srinagar initiated a campaign against prostitution in Maisuma. He was popularly known as

---

[108] ibid
[109] Ibid, p.632
[110] Ibid
[111] Prostitution legal in J&K, government plans to scrap old law, *Indian Express,* 13 May 2006

Muhammad Subhan (hajam)[112]. Subhan, assisted by his friends and several English officials[113] wrote pamphlets highlighting the plight of prostitutes in Kashmir. He would stand up in the streets and preach, and at night, with some of his friends, would stand outside the brothels, preventing the customers from entering them.[114] Through his street shows, Subhan campaigned for returning to prostitutes a normal life[115]. In his bid to close down the brothels, Subhan would stand in front of them with his *dholak*, sing songs and recite self-composed poems, using everyone to refrain from visiting them. In one of his pamphlets, titled *Hajam ki Fariyad*, Subhan says that the state was not co-operating with him and vested elements were creating problems all around. In another pamphlet he gives some insight into the trade. Due to his persuasion, 700 people, including many Kashmiri Pandits and Sikhs supported him and submitted

---

[112] Khan Mohammed Ishaq, *History of Srinagar 1846-1947; A Study in Socio-Cultural Change,* Gulshan Publications, Srinagar, Second Edition, 1999, p.113

[113] One Tyndale Biscoe joined the fray and lent their helping hand to Subhan. He was also able to get the assistance of a police officer whose son had one night been caught by Subhan at the entrance of a brothel. Muhammad Subhan used the good offices of Cannon Biscoe to contact Dr Kathleen Youghan, head of the Kashmir Women Association and apprised her about the tragic sufferings of Kashmiri women. The humane lady contacted the members of the League of Nations and told them about the woeful life of the unfortunate girls.(suhaib matoo, profiling a crusader, *Greater Kashmir*, 18 august 2009)

[114] Cited from Khan Muhammed Ishaq, *History of Srinagar,* p. 113

[115] Mohammed Subhan Hajam, A barber's revolution, *http://jkalternativeviewpoint.com/statenews.php?link=5752*

a memorandum seeking a ban on prostitution to the then district magistrate in Srinagar. After this intense public pressure generated by Subhan, the state Assembly passed the Suppression of Immoral Traffic Act in1934.[116] It provided penalties for persons who kept, managed or allowed the use of any place or a brothel or procured women or girls for prostitution or lived upon the earnings of prostitutes or traffic in women and children. Those who solicited in public places encouraged or abetted seduction or prostitution of minor girls were also penalized."[117] The suppression of immoral Traffic Act of 1934 had a disastrous effect on the lives of the prostitutes, bringing many of them to destitution. It now became difficult for them to eke out their living while some prostitutes made good their escape to places outside Kashmir, there were many who took to charkha (spinning wheel) on Subhan's advice. Sources also refer some that some prostitutes earning a decent living by working in a silk factory.[118]

After the end of the Dogra rule, the prostitution rules stood in place, but since 1947 no prostitute has actually registered herself. [119] Clearly then, the state no longer derives resources by taxing prostitution. However the marginalized women in particular the prostitutes are still under state's surveillance. After Independence, in pursuance of international convention the state In India passed the immoral trafficking (prevention) Act 1956. The Act defines the "prostitution"

---

[116]   Ibid

[117]   J&K *information* (issued by the Bureau of Information, His Highness's Govt., March 1947), pp. 10-11; Census 1941, p.6, cited from Khan Muhammed Ishaq, *History of Srinagar,* p. 113

[118]   Khan, Muhammed Ishaq, *History of Srinagar,* P.116

[119]   ibid

as sexual exploitation or abuse of persons for commercial purposes.[120]

The section2-A of the act " held that any reference in this Act to a law which was not in force in the state of J&K would in relation to that state", be construed as a reference to the corresponding law, if any, in force in that state[121]. The state tried its sex offenders under the prevention of immoral trafficking Act 1956 but the rules of 1921 were not repealed.

The resurgence of violence in the last couple of decades has led to an increase in prostitution, with more and more female victims of violence, poverty and unemployment, taking recourse to prostitution to eke out their living. In the recent decades, the 'Maryiam Squad' of DeM (*Dukhtarane-Millat),* have launched a campaign against the sex workers whose numbers, it claimed, has grown alarmingly in the state[122]. Certain sociologists working on Kashmir have argued that prostitution in Kashmir has fed on the resurgence of violence and conflict in the recent decades. Prof. Bashir Ahmad Dabla, Kashmiri sociologist, terms prostitution in Kashmir as a 'digenerative inferno' and links it to the conflict and violence that has prevailed in Kashmir for more than two decades now[123]. Faced with recurring violence and frequent deaths in the families, Kashmiri women find no protection from the state, and some of them are indeed drawn to prostitution to sustain their families. A notable example

---

[120]   Ibid

[121]   *http://ncpcr.gov.in/Acts/Immoral Traffic Prevention Act (ITPA) 1956.pdf*

[122]   Suri Kavita, *Impact of Violence on Women's Education in Kashmir*, WISCOMP, New Delhi, 2006, p.38

[123]   Ibid

for this come from Dardpora, in Kupwara district, where widowed have either resorted to begging or flesh trade to fulfill their needs[124].

In the debates between mainstream political parties and the separatist leaders, trafficking of women has become a non-issue. 0n 12 May 2006[125], the then law Minister, Muzaffar Hussain Beigh, who was also the Deputy Chief Minister, created a furor when he declared that prostitution was legal in Kashmir. He admitted that though the state tries its sex offenders under the prevention of immoral trafficking Act (PITA) but the sections of its own Ranbir Panel Code have not been repealed[126]. He said that the Rules of 1921 are still published in J&K law books and were still in force[127]. The then, Registrar General of JK high court also, admitted that according to these rules an adult woman could of her own free volition register herself as a prostitute, despite PITA[128].

In July 2006, A lawyer, named, Maulvi Aijaz, who was defending 'rapists' of a Kashmiri girl, claimed that the victim in question was of consenting age and the very law (referring to PITA) on which prosecution was leaning was not applicable to the state. He contended that because of J&K's special status under article 370, the law under which

---

[124]   Ibid, p.38-39

[125]   In 2006, the J&K police unearthed a major sex racket in Srinagar. A ring of 43 girls, two top politicians, 13 police and security force officers were involved in the scam

[126]   http://www.indianexpress.com/news/prostitution-legal-in-J&K-govt-plans-to-scarp.old-law/4334 Accessed on 15 oct 2010

[127]   Ibid

[128]   Ibid

the accused had been booked—Prevention of immoral trafficking Act (PITA)—did not apply as it had not been notified for Kashmir. Aijaz said the victim Yasmeena was actually above 18 and that her family has been practicing prostitution since 1954[129].

These instances of the manipulation of the laws by the defendants reveal an important ambiguity concerning the legal status of prostitution in Kashmir. The origins of this ambiguity clearly go back to the Dogra rule, and it is time now that the state in Kashmir removes it to better protect the lives of marginalized women in the state.

To conclude, under the Dogra rule in Kashmir, prostitution was not only legalized but also actively encouraged by the state. Prostitutes were registered, and the state derived considerable revenues from taxing them. The Prostitution Rules of 1921 legalized prostitution, and required the prostitutes to register with the state. This study has argued that the act brought them within the ambit of state surveillance, allowing the state to oppress and exploit them, and stake a claim over their income and resources. The post-independence period did not see any significant initiative on the part of the state to deal with the problems of the prostitutes. However, the practice of registering prostitutes fell into disuse, but the legal acceptance of prostitution continued, as before. The suppression of immoral traffic act, 1956 was adopted by the state in 1959, but in framing the rules for its adoption, the state did not designate prostitution as illegal. The present study has suggested that this has rendered the position of prostitutes

---

[129] *Times of India*, July 27, 2006

in Kashmir an ambiguous one, in legal terms. It is this legal ambiguity that has prevented both the state and the courts in Kashmir in effectively suppressing the practice. The resurgence of violence in Kashmir has led to a substantial expansion in the number of prostitutes, as violence, poverty and broken homes is driving an increasingly growing number of women to prostitution. But, as a helpless spectator, the state looks on, and is doing nothing!

CHAPTER II

WOMEN IN FAMILY AND COMMUNITY LIFE

Methodology

Even as I have also used secondary data, my study is primarily based on oral interviews and responses to questionnaires[130], circulated to women in Kashmir valley. In the process of the collection of data, informal communication went hand in hand with data collection through formal means. There were a total of 200 respondents equally distributed between towns and villages. There were 100 respondents from the urban centers and another 100 from the villages. They were again sub-divided by class/income with 30% of respondents coming from the upper classes, another 30% from the lower classes and the remaining 40% belonging to the middle classes. All along my

---

[130]   See Appendix-A

effort was to assure them that opinions and responses were both confidential and valuable for me both as a researcher and as a woman.

Family, Kin and Women

The family is, usually seen as a social institution that has come into existence to meet the universal human needs of social and physical reproduction. It is seen in conventional social sciences as a social unit, strengthened by bonds of blood, kin marriage[131]. Influenced by processual thought, several sociologists, such as David Morgan[132] have argued that the family is not an institution, but a set of practices. It is something that we 'do' and not something we are 'in'[133]. The processual approach to family incorporates human agency and subjectivity, but refuse to incorporate socially entrenched beliefs and practices in their understanding of the family. Feminists have challenged the view that under the forces of modernity the family is becoming more egalitarian for women, and argue in contrast, that the family is a site of inequality in which women are subordinated due their position as wives and mothers. Feminists argue that women's position as wives/ mothers results in a position of subordination to men/fathers, at least in part because of economic dependency, but also because of widely shared ideologies of the family.[134]

---

[131] Abbott Pamella, Claire Wallace and Melissa Tyler, *An Introduction to Sociology ; Feminist Perspectives,* Routlegde, London, New York, (3rd edition) 2005, p.145

[132] Morgan D 'Risk and Family Practices', IN E.Silva and C. Smart (eds.), *The New Family,* London Sage, 1999

[133] Abbott Pamella, et.al, *An Introduction to Sociology,* p.145

[134] Ibid., p. 147

In the exchange theory of Claude Levi—Strauss, the human transition from 'nature' to 'culture' was marked by the exchange of women among men.[135] Kinship Systems are characterized by the permanent Circulation of women among men. Levi-Strauss describes women as the 'supreme gift'[136] that is exchanged among men for the maintenance and vitality of kin solidarities[137]. Given the huge influence that kin and community networks still play in India, most marriage are still exchanges between community/kin groups. With the development of the closed, domesticated nuclear families in India, one would have expected a diminishing role of kin and community forces in transactions of marriage. This is, however not the case, and while a relatively small percentage of marriages are made by the choice/preferences of the couples, the bulk of marriages are still conducted by community/kin groups. The revolution in information technology has only made their job easier, and efficient. They use the internet, the newspapers and the magazine to choose the 'right spouse' for their sons and daughters—one who would reinforce their kin/community connections.

The level of subjugation that is exercised over women varies with household composition. Even so, in all family forms, the ideology of patrilineal, patri-virilocal residence governs a woman's life[138].The patrilineal, patri-virilocal joint

---

[135]   Claude-Levi-Strauss, *The Elementary Structures of Kinship,* *tr.* James Harle Bell, John Richard von Strurner and Rodney Needham, Bostan, Beacon Press, 1969, p.64

[136]   [7] Ibid., P. 65

[137]   Ibid., P. 77

[138]   Dube Leela, *Women and Kinship, Comparative Perspectives on Gender in South and South East Asia,* Rawat publications, India

family is far more prevalent among communities engaged in business[139] and the landed groups than among the other social groups.[140] Arguably property helps in maintaining co-residence, although small-scale joint families can indeed function without any property, as well.[141]

A nuclear family may become a 'supplemented nuclear family' or a joint family with the addition of a widowed parent or orphaned siblings or with the marriage of a son, at least for a short period. A stress on conjugality has become an accepted feature of today's family households[142].

The extended family is of two types. The classic extended family is made up of several nuclear families joined by kinship relations. The term is mainly used to describe a situation where many related nuclear families or family members live in the same house, street or area, and the members of these related nuclear families see one another regularly. The modified extended family is one where related nuclear families, although they may be living far apart geographically, nevertheless maintain regular contact and mutual support through regular visits, and communications etc.[143]

  2009 pp.93

[139] Shah A.M, 'Basic Terms and Concepts in the Study of the Family in India', *Indian Economic and Social History Review*, Sage Publication, Vol 1 No.,3. January-March 1964.

[140] Dube Leela, *Women and Kinship*, p.11

[141] Ibid., P. 12

[142] Ibid., P. 13

[143] See for Example, Browne Ken, *An Introduction to Sociology*, Polity Press, UK, 2007 pp.226.

In the Kashmir valley, 'the extended family' is the norm in both rural and urban Kashmir[144]. According to Dabla, the joint families in Kashmir are patrilineal in nature and patrilocal in character[145]. In my survey I came across instances of both 'classic extended families' and 'modified extended families'. The former type is common in rural areas while the latter is common in urban areas even as the growing trend in both villages and towns is towards 'modified extended families'[146]. In Kashmir, the extended family culturally still functions as a close knit single social and economic unit under which adults submit their earnings to the head of the family who is responsible for the fulfillment of the basic requirements for the family. However the extended family system is fast losing its importance in urban areas of Kashmir. According to Scholars based in Kashmir, this is not owing to urbanization and industrialization but is a result of greater preference for autonomy among the urban residents. The desire to move away from extended family and establish a separate closed family unit is more intense among the educated and employed couples.[147] It is clear that there is a considerable diversity in family systems, and all family-types display considerable variations. The extension / Jointness of the families in Kashmir may not be displayed so much by the outward symbols like co-residence, but it continues to

---

[144] Muhammed Dost & Bhat. A.S., 'Family in Kashmir' IN (ed.) Gulshan Majeed, *Look n Kashmir From Ancient and Modern,* Jay Kay Books Srinagar 2006.P.62

[145] Dabla B.A., *Sociological Papers on Kashmir,* Volume- 2, Jay Kay publishers, 2010, p.264

[146] Based on the observation in Field Survey by the Researcher in between 2009-2010

[147] Dost Muhammad and Bhat A.S., 'Family in Kashmir', p.64

survive through emotional bondage, privilege inheritance and obligations within kinship and/or community network of relations. Sociologists call this 'functional solidarity' of the joint family which does not disappear with occupational diversification and geographical dispersion of its members.

Studies in Kashmir so far, have shown that members of the nuclear families also depend heavily on their parents in times of stress, particularly at the time of child birth and a crisis in the family[148]. There is a division of household chores and both men and women share the burden of household chores. Presumably, women in rural areas shoulder greater burden of responsibilities than women living in urban centers. They look after children, take care of domestic animals, collect cow dung and fuel wood from nearby woodlands and forest, fetch drinking water, wash clothes, cook food and help men in the fields. In contrast women in urban areas have less household chores-washing, cooking and looking after the children[149]. The early lessons of gender—dictated roles are taught in families when domestic chores are divided amongst children on this basis. Boys and girls are encouraged to grow in separate environments with different roles and expectations. As mentioned above, women in rural areas perform multiple roles which call for less confinement.

The average size of the family in the 19th century, as it appears from Lawrence's report[150], was seven. It appears to have remained the same when the census reports were

---

[148]   Ibid, p. 62
[149]   ibid
[150]   Lawrence was writing in 1887

published in 1981[151]. According to my field survey the average family size is approx.6.15. Normally in rural areas the average size of the joint families was 9 and that of nuclear families was 5. The size of joint families in urban areas was 7 for joint families and for nuclear families 5. (See Tables II (a) and II (b)

Table II (a) Family Size in Rural Kashmir

Size	4	2	6	5	8	14	11	9	10	12	5	7	3
Number	15	1	20	18	8	2	4	9	3	2	2	14	2

Source: Field Work by the Researcher

Table II (b) Family Size in Urban Kashmir

Size	7	3	9	4	6	10	13	5	8
Number	14	8	2	23	14	4	1	29	5

Source: Field Work by the Researcher.

Interestingly a study has suggested that the size of family varies not with economic status but with the level of education in the family. The more educated families have fewer children and are thus smaller in size whereas the less educated and illiterate families usually much larger in size[152]. The number of children and the size of family

---

[151] Cited from, Dost Muhammad & Bhat A.S 'Family in Kashmir' p.62

[152] Ibid

is usually smaller among working families, in particular among families where both parents are working compared to families which are engaged in business or farming[153]. During my interactions with the women in Kashmir, I found that though the number of nuclear families is on the increase, the affinal ties, and regular exchange of gifts and invitations for feasts are still particularly strong in Kashmir.[154] The subordinate position of women in the family and the violence—physical, verbal and symbolic, that women suffer in their families is reflected in Kashmiri folk literature. Conjugal incompatibility and the role of extended family members in women's subjugation in family is also evident in Kashmiri folk songs as well. [155] The relations between *Hash*(mother-in-law) and *Nosh*(daughter-in-law) are portrayed as discordant in the bulk of folk songs, and in a few songs where their relations is described as cordial, it is still portrayed as one of doubt and distrust.

> *'Hash ti thez nosh ti thez*
> *Deg dez vali kus'*

(Since both mother-in-law and daughter in law equally claim high pedigree, none is ready to remove a boiling pot from the burning stove which s ready to be spoilt)

> *'Nosh bemie phoher*
> *Hashi demi budith'*

---

[153] Ibid p.61,62

[154] Kaw. M.K, *Kashmir and Its People Studies in the Evolution of Kashmiri Society.*APH Publishing Corporation, New Delhi, India, 2004, p. 313-314

[155] Farooq Fayaz *Folklore and History of Kashmir* Nunaposh Publications Srinagar 2002, p. 122

(Remember, daughter-in-law I have given you a spoilt food I know, o my mother-in-law, I will pay you in the same coin when you grew old and grey)[156]

The relationship between *Zaam* and *baikakiny* (sister-in law and bride) as depicted in Kashmiri folk literature is no less strained and conflict laden. At times the relation between the two is presented in a manner as predicating disintegration of the Kashmiri family life. There is a Kashmiri proverb that says:-

"Zam hei asi gam teti peth sozes pam"

(How does it matter, if zam is married distant away, she will seldom miss an opportunity to tease her sister-in-law?)[157]

Domestic Labour:

In India, a woman is identified with the household, and is supposed to have no existence outside her family. She is expected to look after the household affairs, and has no existence at least for most men other than as a wife or/and a mother. In the perception of people, household affairs like bearing and rearing of children are associated with womanhood. In the financially well-off household, women get some help from domestic servants (to whom they conveniently pass off their burden) but they are expected

---

[156] Dabla B.A, *Socio-logical Papers on Kashmir*, Vol-1, JAYKAY Books, Srinagar, 2010, p. 126

[157] Ibid., p. 130

to run the household and rear the children properly.[158]In my field study, in Kashmir province, 62 out of 200(31%) respondents admitted taking the help of a maid either occasionally, or on regular basis. Among these only 34(17%) respondents were regularly enjoying the assistance of a maid servant for carrying out the daily household chores. Figure 2.1, illustrates the extent of the use of domestic labour among Kashmiri families. It is evident from the data, based on fieldwork, and that urban women are assisted by domestic labourers, in carrying out their daily household chores more often than is the case with the women in the villages.

Feminists have argued that the domestic labour is physically and emotionally demanding work, but is rarely recognized as such. They often point out that it is women who are generally responsible for the choices of daily life, repetitive and monotonous, whereas men engage in activities that are both economically productive, and for the higher class men at least, also emotionally satisfying. The division of labour is based on what men and women are thought to be naturally good at. Women are thought to be naturally good at cleaning, sewing, washing up, shopping, caring for children, cooking and so on.[159] Ann Oakley has pointed out that even when conjugal roles are shared, men are generally said to be 'helping' their wives.[160] Even when wives have paid employment and jobs of their own, they still continue domestic work-, performing, what feminists term as 'the dual role'. In recent years, feminists have recognized that many

---

[158] Mishra Saraswati, *Status of Indian Women,* Gyan Publishing House, New Delhi 2002 p.114

[159] Abbot Pamella et.al (ed.), Op.cit, p.164

[160] See for example; Oakley. A. *Subject Women* London, Fontana, 1982

women actually undertake a 'triple shift' not only working outside of the home, as well as taking responsibility for the performance of domestic labour, but also providing care and assistance to elderly or dependent family members as well[161].

Fig 2.1   Domestic Servants in Kashmiri Households

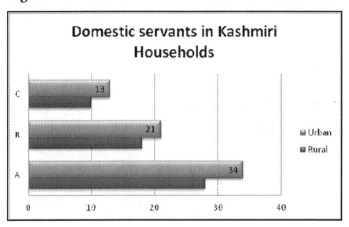

A: Total No. of households hiring servants

B: No. of families hiring domestic servants on a permanent basis

C: No. of families hiring domestic servants on an intermittent basis.

Source: Field Work by the Researcher (The findings are based on the oral interviews of 200 respondents conducted by the researcher)

---

[161]   Abbot Pamella et.al, *An Introduction to Sociology*, p. 164

In my field survey in Kashmir, about 44% of my total respondents admitted that their spouses assisted them in the domestic chores. This help was in most of the cases occasional and was restricted to the period of illness or pregnancy. It is interesting to note here that men in urban areas helped their wives more often than those living in villages.[162] 24% men in urban areas helped their wives in household activities as against 20% men in the rural areas. There is of course a class dimension here, as well. The upper class men—in both the towns and the villages-are less likely to help their spouses, than men lower in class and rank. [163]

Discrimination against women in the family:

The Kashmiri society is a tradition-bound society. As is the case with many traditional societies in Asia, there prevails widespread and deep rooted discrimination against the female sex in the Kashmiri society[164]. In a survey Dabla revealed that about 63% women respondents felt that there was widespread discrimination against women.[165]

---

[162] Such families are mostly nuclear families or a single woman household.

[163] (Family income; Upper Class: 5,00000-10,00000, and above; Middle class: 1,50000 to 5,00000; Lower class: below 1,50000)

[164] Dabla Bashir Ahmad, Sandeep.K.Nayak, Khurshid-ul-Islam, *Gender Discrimination In the Kashmir Valley; A Survey of Budgam and Baramulla Districts*, Gyan Publications, Delhi, 2000 pp.91

[165] Dabla Bashir Ahmad, *Domestic Violence Against Women In Kashmir Valley*, JAYKAY publications, Srinagar, 2009 p 18

Education

Women and girls receive far less education than men, due to social norms but also increasingly owing to fears of violence.

As is evident from the census data (Table II c) the women's literacy in Kashmir as everywhere else in India is lagging behind men's literacy. However the situation seems to have changed since 1961. Women's literacy rate rose from 20% in 1981 to 48% in 2011, an increase of 28%. With women's literacy standing at 58.1% in 2011, the percentage increase in the two decades following 1981 comes to 10.1% lowered down.[166]

Table II(c) Literacy Rate 1961-2011

	Literacy Rate (In Percentage)		
Year	**Persons**	**Males**	**Females**
1961	12.95	19.75	5.05
1971	12.71	31.01	10.94
1981	33.02	44.55	19.86
1991	N.A	N.A	N.A
2001	55.52	66.60	43.00
2011	68.74	78.26	58.01

Source; Census of India, J&K, 2011 (Provisional) *www.censusofindia.com*

---

[166] Census of India, J&K, 2011 (Provisional) *http://censusindia.gov.in/ accessed on 15 November 2011*

In his study, Dabla, revealed that for a vast majority of women, education did not go beyond the three R's, and very few among them took to education for professional reasons.[167] The school dropout rate is higher among female students, as compared to the male students. Further, the rate of female dropout is higher at the primary level than the middle/secondary levels of education. There seems according to Dabla least discrimination against the female children in sending them to primary school[168].

In my study, a little more than half the respondents—101 out of 200 respondents—confirmed that their families did not want to see them educated, and favored their brothers over them when it came to education. Several women in general responded that their families would have been interested in our education if only they exhibited the willingness or the ability to learn. They held themselves responsible for their illiteracy and not their families. On the other hand 43% of urban respondents felt that their families discriminated with them in giving them the necessary education. The discrimination was felt greater in the case of the middle and the lower classes of the population. 42 out of 60 lower class respondents noted that they were discriminated against while 41 out of 80 respondents from the middle class were discriminated against at the time when they were seeking education. Only 10 out of 60 respondents from the upper classes had similar feelings. (See fig 2.2)

---

[167] Dabla, *Multidimensional Problems*, p.123
[168] Ibid., p. 129,130

Fig 2.2   Class Based Patterns of Discrimination against Women in Education.[169]

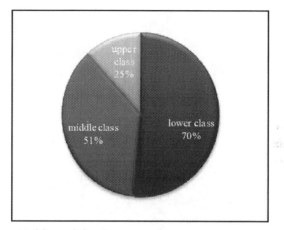

Source: Field Work by the researcher.

---

[169]   Note; The respondents in the above sample belonged to the middle age group(above 25), therefore the data depicts the situation more than 20 years now in Kashmir.

Food, Nutrition and Basic Health Facilities

Nutrition is one of the significant axes of gender differentiation in South Asia. A number of empirical studies have presented this bitter truth about Bangladesh, India and Pakistan[170]. When resources are scarce this discrimination can be acute, and girls may remain underfed and undernourished.[171]

B.A.Dabla, in his study, found that 24% women in Kashmir felt that they were discriminated against in matters of food and nutrition[172]. As against this, my study revealed that 5 out of 200 respondents experienced discrimination at the hands of their families in food and nutrition (**Table 3.4**). No such case was recorded among the upper and the middle classes. All 5 belonged to the lower class.

Discrimination in food and nutrition	Upper classes (60)	Lower lower (60)	Middle classes (80)
Yes	-	5	-
No	60	55	78
Can't say	-	—	2

Table 3.4

Source: Field Work by the Researcher

---

[170] Dube Leela, *Women and Kinship.*, p.137

[171] Ibid

[172] Dabla, *Domestic Violence Against Women in Kashmir Valley,* JAY KAY publications, 2010 Srinagar, p- 19

The lack of concern for women's health is reflected in the large number of facilities during women's pregnancy and childbirth. Every year, about 6,000 mothers die in childbirth and allied complications of pregnancy[173]. India's maternal mortality rate (MMR) stands at 450 per 100,000 live births, against 540 in 1998-1999[174]. As per the study conducted in September by the team led by Dr. Meenakshi Jha from the Centre for Disease Control and Prevention, in the four districts of J&K, 357 women of reproductive age(15-49) died, and 154 died of complications during pregnancy childbirth or the puerperal period[175]. MMR in those 4 districts was 418 in Kupwara, 774 in Islamabad, 2182 in Baramulla, and 6507 in Bandipora. Baramulla district showed the highest mortality risk ever recorded human history, with 54% more than half of the women of reproductive age—during 1998 and 2003[176]. The causes included hemorrhage, obstructed labour, cardiomyopathy, sepris, obstetric embolism and pregnancy—induced hypertension, whereas indirect causes were tuberculosis malaria, and obstetric tetanus. 60% Kashmiri do not have access to basic health services. Most of the professional cares are used by only 20% of all pregnant women. [177]

---

[173] Kashmir: Where women die giving birth, *http://www. greaterKashmir.com/news/2010/Nov/4/Kashmir-where-women-die-giving-birth-30.asp* Accessed on 18-5-2011

[174] Ibid

[175] Ibid

[176] Ibid

[177] Ibid

Choice of Career:

In South Asia women are mostly denied the freedom to choose their profession. Their choice is mainly constrained by the society[178]. Kashmir is no exception there. In my study I found that about 35% (69/200) of women believed that their choice of career was constrained by their families[179].

Even though their choice is constrained but it seems women have not stopped participating in economic activities in Kashmir. Apart from maintaining their traditional roles, and their participation in traditional economic sectors, women in Kashmir, have joined new and upcoming professions, as well[180]. Aneesa Shafi has in her study found that the choice of profession for women in Kashmir was severely restricted to teaching in schools to colleges.[181] My enquiry, in contrast to the Aneesa Shafi's work, revealed that only 10% of families prefer teaching professions for their women. Table II(d) reveals, the bulk of the remaining families actually did not have a career choice for their women.

---

[178] Dube Leela, *Women and Kinship*, p. 56

[179] Field Survey by the Researcher between 2009-2010

[180] Dabla Bashir Ahmad, *Sociological Papers on Kashmir*, Vol.1, JAYKAY Publications, Srinagar, p.205

[181] Aneesa Shafi, *Working Women In Kashmir; Problems and Prospects,* APH publications, Delhi, 2002, p.55

Table II (d): Professions favoured for women in Kashmir

Profession favoured	Urban(100)	Rural(100)
Teacher	8	12
Med.doc	4	4
Any	87	84
None.	1	0

Source: Field Work by the Researcher

Sports and Outdoor Activities

In my study, 27% women said that they were not allowed to participate in the sports and outdoor activities in their families. 18% rural women and 36% of urban women shared this feeling. Thus it is evident **(see fig 2.3)** here that women in urban areas were more confined and secluded than those living in villages. Among the urbanites, seclusion of women is practiced far more among middle and upper class families, than the lower class families.

Discrimination in Inheritance:

According to Dabla customary laws in Kashmir, especially those related to inheritance rights of women before or after their marriage, represent a clear case of discrimination against women here[182]. Like in other areas of life, Muslim women, in practice, get discriminated in getting their inheritance

---

[182] Dabla, *Sociological Papers,* Vol.1, p.206

rights granted to them in the Islamic Shari at[183]. According to Dabla's findings, about 55% of women in Kashmir have been denied their inheritance rights in property[184].

In my survey I observed that 45(22.5%) women out of 200 respondents received some property from their natal families. While in urban areas 19 out of 100 respondents received property by inheritance, their number in the villages, with the number of respondents remaining the same, was 26. Among the upper classes 20 out of 60 women (33.3%), and among the middle classes, 18 out of 80 women (22.5%) received inheritable rights in property, (**See fig.2.4).**

---

[183]   Dabla, *Multidimensional Problems of Women*, 2007, p.89
[184]   Ibid

Fig 2.3   Discrimination in Sports and out-door activities.

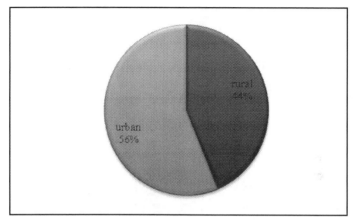

Source: Field Work by the Researcher.

Fig 2.4   Discrimination in Inheritance Rights.

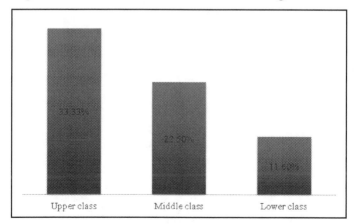

Source: Field Work by the Researcher

Son Preference

Sociological studies have shown that in our society, bound by traditions and patriarchy, sons are usually considered an 'asset' and daughters as 'liability' to the family. The preference for a male child is an age old practice in Indian families.

The sex ratio data available in the census reports reveals two distinctive trends. Firstly, the Post-independence period was marked by a stable growth in the sex ratio in favor of women, indicating an improvement in women's position in the society. Secondly, the disturbed conditions in the recent decades reflect in the decline in sex-ratio, suggesting a correlation between the secessionist violence and the position of women in Kashmir. See fig 2.5 and table II (e).

Table II (e); Sex-ratio in the J&K state since 1901

Year	Sex ratio
1901	882
1911	876
1921	870
1931	865
1941	869
1951	873
1961	878
1971	878
1981	892
1991	892
2001	892
2011	883

Source: Census of India, J&K, 2011(Provisional)

Fig 2.5   Sex Ratio in J&K from 1901 to 2011

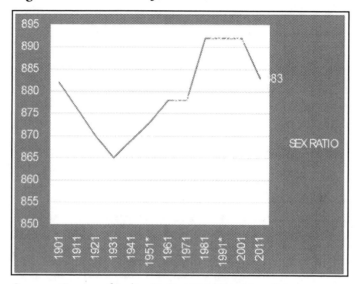

Source: Census of India, J&K, 2011(Provisional)
http://censusindia.gov.in/

Seclusion After marriage

Purdah or the seclusion of women is closely related to the concern over management of female sexuality characteristic of south Asia. All over south-Asia *Purdah* among Muslims is justified by the reference to Islam. Although interpretations of Quranic verses vary and several Muslim feminists have argued that Islam does not prescribe seclusion for women, the common understanding is that *Purdah* has religious sanction.[185].

Until the 19th century the dress of people in Kashmir, both male and female, commonly consisted of long loose wrapper (*Pheran*) and trousers. Reflecting the changing concerns with the correlations between apparel and masculinity, the 1930s saw in Kashmir, a movement led, among others, by one Pandit Kashyap Bandhu, against men donning *pheran*, which, it was thought, was an effeminate dress.[186]. The usual headdress for little girls was skull caps. After marriage, a Muslim girl would have, as her headgear a thicker turban like red cap (*qasaba*) 'studded with innumerable pins and over it a spare of country cloth (*pooch*) to act, in the case of necessity, as a veil which also usually covered the whole back.[187] The Pundit women's headgear was known as *Taranga*. Contacts with the Women in the plains however brought about many changes in the mode of dress of the Kashmiri women. The *qasaba* and *tarnaga* have largely disappeared, and have largely been replaced with north-Indian dresses, in particular,

---

[185]   Dube Leela, *Women and Kinship*, p. 60,

[186]   Bazaz P.N. *Daughters of Vitasta; A History of Kashmiri Women from Early Times to the Present Day.* Pamposh Publications, 1959, p.250

[187]   Ibid p.199

shalwar and *chudidar pyjama*, and frock.[188] The *saree* had also become quite a fad among upper class Pundit women.[189] The ordinary veil worn by the Kashmiri women was called *burqa*.[190] It consisted of a long piece of cotton cloth thrown over the head and allowed to hang down the back. Its use was confined to the Muslims alone. However, the working class Muslim women like *Hanjis*(Fisher community) and *Watals* (scheduled castes) did not wear the *burqa*.[191] In my field survey, I found that most of the women observed *purdah* though in variety of forms. According to my data, about 73% of women observe *purdah*. And the trend was more or less same in rural as well as urban areas. 71 out of 100 (71%) urban respondents observed *purdah,* whereas among the rural women, their number was 75 out of 100 (75%).

Table II(f) Women Observing *Purdah*

Class	Number	Total	Percentage
Upper class	36	60	60
Middle Class	57	80	71
Lower class	52	60	86.6

Source: Field Work by the Researcher

---

[188] ibid p. 252-253, also see Khan, Muhammed Ishaq, *History of Srinagar,* p.97

[189] Census 1931, I, p.102 cited from Khan Muhammed Ishaq, *History of Srinagar,* p.97

[190] Tyndale Biscoe, C.E., *Kashmir in Sunlight and Shade*, Lippincott, 1922, p.150;

[191] census 1921, I, p.90 Cf. Khan Muhammed Ishaq, *History of Srinagar,* p. 98

The family, and the husband as its head, played a crucial role in enforcing dress restrictions on women. In my survey I found that 43% of married women in villages, and 54% in the urban centers, were observing *purdah* owing to the instructions of their spouses. While *purdah* is indeed observed by the bulk of Kashmiri women, it is only 49% among them, who actually don the *burqa*. In all other cases, a chador to cover the body, as even a *duppata* to cover the head would suffice as fulfilling the requirements of *purdah*.

Table II (g) Types of *Veiling* In Kashmir

Type of veiling	*Burqa*		Covering head with *duppata*		*Chador*		
	No.	Percentage	No.	Percentage	No.	Percentage	Total
Number of women	77	49.3	71	45.5	8	5.1	156

Source: Field Work by the Researcher

Restriction on women's movement:

Out of the total 200 women respondents that I interviewed 72 women admitted to strict restrictions on their movement. The surveillance of the husband over his wife was a common element in both the urban and rural societies. [192]

---

[192]   Data collected by the Researcher from 2009 to 2010.

Marriage, household and Women:-

Leela Dube firmly asserts that marriage is a desired aspiration for nearly all women in Bangladesh, India, Nepal, and Pakistan. Among Hindus marriage sacralizes and sanctifies female sexuality, while Islam wholly disapproves of sex outside marriage. Since sex is viewed as a natural craving of human beings, marriage is visualized as an event that is necessary part of life, particularly for women[193].

In Kashmir, most marriages are arranged by the respective families. Usually once the parents decide to marry of their children, a go-between, called *manzim yor* in local parlance, is approached to find a suitable match from a family of identical social status and background[194]. The middlemen, who maintain lists of prospective brides and bridegrooms, play crucial roles in arranging marriages in the society. Only a small number of marriages, particularly between cousins, are arranged without the involvement of middle men. In such marriages the proposal usually comes from the side of the groom. It is not customary for the parents of a girl to make a marriage proposal even when the boy is a near relation.[195].

Marriages are usually treated as sacred occasions, and are, therefore, followed with a number of sacred rituals.[196]. The marriage involves the signing of marriage contract, *Nikahnama* between the principals. The *Nikahnama* is

---

[193]   Dube.Leela, *Women and Kinship* pp.109
[194]   Dost Muhammed and Bhat A.S., 'Family in Kashmir' *p.66*
[195]   Ibid p.67
[196]   Ibid.,

prepared after the principals' consent to the marriage, unambiguously, in presence of a representative (*vakil*)[197] and two witnesses *(shahids)* who represents them before the *moulvi* and sign the *nikahnama* on their behalf. The *vakil* and the *shahid* are always the near relations of contracting marriage partners[198]. Marriage being a contract, either of the parties should be able to set conditions for the same[199], but, as scholars like N.J.Caulson and A.A.Fyzee, point out, it is perceived that the Islamic law does not accept an unrestricted liberty of contract, for that would be incompatible with ethical control of conjugal relations[200]. The persons engaging to tie the conjugal knot are, however, permitted to enter stipulations in the marriage contract, provided they are in accordance with the rights and duties of spouses, as arranged for in *shari'a.* The *Nikahnama* also mentions the sum of *Mahr* or dower that the bridegroom pledges to pay to the bride before consummation of marriage. The amount is invariably fixed in accordance with the socio-economic status of the families concerned. However there are some unique rituals and celebrations before and on the day of ceremony of a Kashmiri marriage. They are not religiously significant but direct the conjugal rights and relation more explicitly. After a marriage proposal is agreed upon by the families, celebration begins with the betrothal of the principals. On the day of betrothal, the parents of the bride-to-be arrange a lavish feast for the family members and guests invited by the parents

---

[197] Dost Mohammed translates the word Vakil here as Agent, which does not connote the actual meaning

[198] ibid

[199] ibid

[200] See for example; Caulson N.J. *Succession in the Muslim Family,* Cambridge University Press, UK, 1971, also see; .Fyzee A.A, *Outlines of Muhammadan Law,* Fourth Edition, New Delhi,1999

of the prospective bridegroom. The girl is shown to female guests and near relatives of the boy who present her with gifts and cash. Crystalline loaf sugar (*Nabad*) is exchanged by the mothers of the boy and the girl and is called *Nabad Nishain* (lit; 'engagement'). Another form of betrothal, called *Nikah Nishain*, is more ceremonious and on the occasion of the betrothal, a number of gold ornaments and gold coins are presented to the bride by the parents, relatives and friends of the bridegroom. After a couple of weeks the parents of the bride send gifts to the bridegroom, his parents and other close relatives.[201] The betrothal including *Nikah* does not confer any conjugal rights on the couple unless their marriage is solemnized. The formalities for solemnizing the marriage begin with the exchange of documents (*saatnama*), specifying the marriage details between the families. The process is initiated by the family of the bridegroom but the day is fixed by the parents of the bride. If the *Nikah* is not completed earlier, it is performed on the occasion of the solemnization of the marriage[202]. The husband retains residence in his residence in his parental home and the wife settles there with his parents. In some cases, the husband lives with his wife in her parental home *(Garepeth zamtur)* along with her parents and sisters, if any. However the later practice, which was quite common in olden days, is not preferred these days by either of the spouses[203].

---

[201] Dost Muhammed and Bhat A.S., 'Family in Kashmir' p.67

[202] Ibid., p. 68-69

[203] Ibid 70

Age at Marriage

Despite the legal prohibition, as is well-known, child marriages are frequent occurrences in India. The rate of child marriages is quite substantial in several states of India, in Particular, Bihar (17.6%), Madhya Pradesh (15.4%) Rajasthan (14.8%) and Dadra and Nagar Haveli (14.3%), west Bengal (14.8%). The record of Kashmir in this matter is much better[204]. In Jammu and Kashmir 0.2% of total marriages are child marriages and 35.2% of total marriages are conducted before the girl completed 18 years of age. 11 districts in Jammu and Kashmir had no record of child marriages. These included Anantnag, Budgam, Baramulla, Kupwara, Pulwama, of Kashmir Province. There was no marriage below 18 years recorded in Kupwara and Pulwama. It was also observed that in Jammu and Kashmir 50% of the total marriages reported were 20 plus age group marriages.[205]

Scholars now suspect that delayed marriages are becoming a norm in Kashmir. The average age of late marriage in present milieu, as observed by Dabla, is 31.53 for men and 27.83 for women [206] The late marriages in Kashmir reflect the socio-economic crisis in Kashmir, and the growing unemployment, which prevents them from setting up their independent households. .

---

[204]   Devi Radha, 'Timing of Marriage in India, Vision and *Reality*', IN, Kamal K.Misra, Janet Huber Lowry,(ed.), *Recent Studies on Indian Women Emperical Work of Social Scientists,* Rawat Publications, 2007, p. 109-122

[205]   Ibid

[206]   Dabla, Bashir Ahmad, *Sociological Papers*, Vol 2, p.372

Authority of Choice in marriages:

William J. Goode, while discussing the Freedom of choice in Indian marriages has pointed out that the freedom of choice presupposes a relatively adult age at marriage and a system of courtship where individual has the time and opportunity to know the variety of potential spouses before making a choice[207].

In my survey I found that the marriages are mostly arranged by the families. Very few women marry according to their choice. 33 among 200 women (16%) respondents said they had married by choice. The occurrence of love marriages was less common in lower classes (7%), when compared to middle and upper urban classes where the number of love marriages was 19% and 24% respectively. See figures (3.6 and 3.7).

---

[207] Goode, J.William, *World Revolutions and Family Patterns*, Collier Macmillan, New York 1963

Fig 2.6 Choice in Marriage

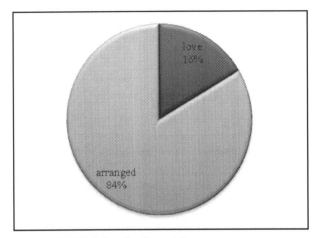

Source: Field Work by the Researcher

Fig 2.7 Love Marraiges in Kashmir

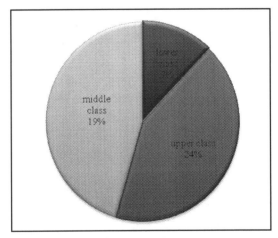

Source: Field Work by the Researcher

Dowry:

Various anthropological studies, particularly of north Indian Marriage and kinship patterns, emphasis that, hyper-gamous unions lead to more or less permanent asymmetry in gift—giving and receiving. This further gives rise to a Continuous flow of gifts or items from bride's family. In a way the in-marrying girl is also viewed as a property of husband if not of the conjugal family. Dowry is nothing less than a form of property in which members of the family, both men and women, have different interests and control.[208]

The Dowry prohibition Act,1961 (amendment till date from time to time) defines dowry as " any property or valuable security given or agreed to be given either directly or indirectly—(a) by one party to a marriage to other party to the marriage; or (b) by the parents of either party to a marriage or by any other person or after the marriage or to any other person; at or before or after marriage in connection with the marriage of the said parties, but does not include dower or *mahar* in the case of persons to whom the Muslim Personal Law (shariat) applies. In Jammu and Kashmir, the Dowry Restraint Act, 1960 has been passed which can be described as a cogent Act of the above piece of legislation[209].

In Kashmir dowry was practically non-existent among the Muslims. Khan, points out, that the system of dowry among the *Musalmans* of Srinagar dates back to the days of Bakshi

---

208   Sharma urrula, *Dowry in North India ;Its Consequences For Women* IN R.Hirschon(ed.) Women and poverty; Women as property, London Croon helm, 1984, p. 62-64

209   Afzal Wani, *Kashmir University Law Review*, 1996 p.72-82

Ghulam Muhaammed former Prime Minister of the J&K state, when families received untold money and favours from the ruling party and gave dowry in order to move up in the social hierarchy.[210] Among pundits the system of dowry had almost attained the force of law.[211] And this was despite the rapid progress of western education among the pundits; for a young man who had done well at college was a most desirable bridegroom, and the price tended to rise as steadily as the demand.

According to Dabla the practice of dowry is certainly in vogue in the Kashmir valley. According to an estimate, dowry was prevalant in 62.08% of the marriages taking place in Kashmir.[212]

In my survey, I found that 43 women among a total of 200 held that their in-laws have derided them for not bringing a handsome dowry either emotionally or physically or both. The dowry demands were more in urban (22%) families than in rural families (16%). Further in urban areas there was a total absence of dowry in upper class families, and even in rural areas only 2 women had experienced it. More women (23/60), 38% from the lower classes have been tortured for dowry than the women coming from better-off sections of society. (fig 2.8)

---

[210] Cf. Khan Muhammed Ishaq, *History of Srinagar,* p. 114
[211] ibid
[212] Dabla, B.A, *Multi-dimensional Problems of Women,* p. 70-73

Fig 2.8 Class based Pattern of Dowry Demand

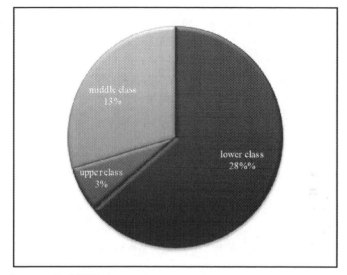

Source: Field Work

Divorce and Remarriages:

Divorces in Kashmir are rare, and there is a lot of social stigma attached to the practice. Despite the moral repugnance, divorces do take place in Kashmir. After getting divorce, the Muslim women in Kashmir can easily marry again, provided she is of a marriageable age[213]. Remarriage is not a taboo in Kashmir. Usually both men and women divorcees remarry or at least intend to marry again. The remarriage of men and women among other factors also depends on the number and age of children at the time of divorce, economic situation of the persons involved, educational and social status of the persons involved and family background. Generally the widow remarriage is acceptable and favorable in the Kashmiri society[214].

Domestic Violence

Gender violence occurs throughout the world, but it take different forms in different social contexts. It is located in particular set of social relationship, structures of power, and meanings of gender[215]. Although enhanced gender equality is commonly thought to diminish gender violence, more egalitarian societies are still plagued by widespread gender

---

[213] Dabla et.al., *Gender Discrimination in the Kashmir Valley,* p., 427-429

[214] Ibid

[215] Sally Engle Merry, *"Gender Violence; A Cultural Perspective: Introductions to Engaged Anthropology.* Wiley-Blackwell, 2009pp.3-4

violence. Traditional or rural societies are not symmetrically more violent than modern or urban ones[216].

Studies all over the world report gender violence, but it is very difficult to develop any numerical measure of its frequency.[217]Between 1967 and 1973, battering men killed over 1750 American women and children. Nearly 60% of the women killed in the US die in the hands of their husbands or boyfriends.[218] Domestic violence is Systematic and structural. It is a reflection of unequal relationships sustained by patriarchy built on male superiority and female inferiority, sex stereotyped roles, expectations and economic social and political predominance of men and dependency of women[219]. According to chairperson of the State Women's Commission Shameema Firdous Domestic violence against them has shown a spurt over the past 20 years. A total of 2000 cases were registered with the commission, out of which 500 were disposed off. As many as 800 cases of marital discords were received from Kashmir while 700 such cases were received from Jammu.[220]

---

[216] Ibid

[217] Ibid 20-21

[218] Ahlawat Neerja, "Violence Against Women: Voices from the Field" in Manjit Singh and D.P Singh (Ed.), *Violence: Impact and Intervention.* Atlantic Publication, New Delhi 2008, p.-141-142

[219] Ibid, p. 151

[220] http://www.dnaindia.com/india/report_jammu-and-Kashmir-women-s-commission-chief-bats-for-introduction-of-women-s-reservation-bill_1367299Sunday, April 4, 2010, accessed on may 4 2010

The prevalence of any domestic violence (physical or sexual) is least in Himachal Pradesh, at 6 percent, followed by Jammu and Kashmir (13 percent) and Goa (15 percent). Any violence is most common in Bihar (56 percent), followed by Rajasthan, Madhya Pradesh, and Tripura (45-47 percent)[221].

Wife battering is institutionalized and has familial sanctions. It ranges from beating, kicking, slapping, accusing, verbal abuse, finding faults in domestic work, long unending working hours within and outside home, denial of good health care, etc. There are a growing number of cases being registered under section 498A of the Penal Code (IPC,1983) which indicts a husband or relative of the husband for cruelty against a wife. It has also been argued that it is not a women's dependence which makes her vulnerable[222]. A wife having a high position job may be beaten more often than her unemployed counterpart. Wife battering is a reflection of power relationship between husband and wife. It has been observed that women not only accept the violence of their spouse as routine, but also often blame themselves for it. It was also observed that there was wide tolerance for wife abuse and it was considered legitimate under certain conditions like neglect of household duties, dowry demands not fulfilled, not obeying the dictates of husband etc.[223]

In Kashmir my field survey in the revealed about 29% of women suffered domestic violence. Out of 200 women 58 accepted that they were beaten by their husbands. Among rural women, my survey revealed, about 30%(30/100)

---

[221] *http://www.measuredhs.com/pubs/pdf/FRIND3/15Chapter15.pdf*
[222] Ahlawat Neerja, *Violence Against Women* p.149-151
[223] Ibid

suffered domestic violence; the percentage of women suffering domestic violence in urban centers stood at 28%(28/100). It would seem from the small margin of the difference that the abuse of women in households was largely unaffected by the urban: rural divide, see figure 2.9 and table II(h).

Table II (h) Wife Battering in Kashmir

Responses	Number
Sometimes/	33
frequently	8
In the past	17
Can't say	2

Source: Field Work

Fig 2.9   Wife Battering in Kashmir

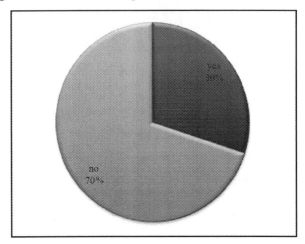

Source: Field Work by the Researcher

Fig 2.10   Class based pattern of Wife beating in Kashmir

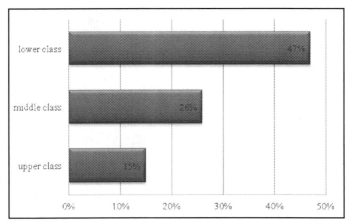

Source: Field Work by the Researcher

In the (fig 2.10) it is clear that upper class women are also victims of spouse beating but their number is higher in case of middle and lower class women. The practice seems to be more common in rural uneducated women. Most field studies of domestic violence reveal that women, having internalized patriarchal norms, often do not perceive themselves as abused unless they have suffered severe physical assault[224]. Further women themselves have perception of an their social roles in society, and more importantly, of their inadequacies in fulfilling them. In a conversation with my respondents a significant number of women admitted that they were beaten by their spouses sometimes but was often followed by attempts to justify it. One of the women who accepted the fact that her husband sometimes beats her added that the beating is not severe but mild and includes mainly slapping. She further added that whenever she was beaten by her spouse it was owing to her own fault. In her words *meani chi galti asan tawai chi layan*(he beats be only when I am wrong) and *Khandaras chu haqh galti paeth layenuk* (Husband has a right to beat his wife when she does something wrong). In the NFHS—3 findings it has been revealed that the proportion of women who have experienced only physical violence, as well as those who have experienced both physical and sexual violence, or have experienced physical or sexual violence, increases with age till the age group 30-39, but then declines somewhat for the older age group. Sexual violence only does not increase linearly with

---

[224]   Sobha Venkatesh Ghosh, 'Contextualizing Domestic Violence: Family Community, State', in Rinki Bhattacharya *Behind Close Doors, Domestic violence in India* Sage Publications New Delhi p.59

age and is highest for women in the age-groups 15-19 and 20-24[225].

An old aged women from a rural uneducated background admitted that when they were young her husband would beat her sometimes but then she quickly added that it was all out of love. She added that in a married life it is a blessing and said *taeth layenus ti aus panun maza* (beating by a husband is sweet in its own ways).

A bill to protect women in Jammu and Kashmir from domestic violence was introduced in the legislative Assembly on 26 March 2010[226]. The bill defines 'domestic violence' to include actual abuse or threats by husbands that is physical, sexual, verbal, emotional or economic. Harassment by way of dowry demands would also be covered under the definition. According to the objectives of the bill, the measure seeks to 'protect the women from being victims of domestic violence in society and cover those women who are in a relationship with the abuser where both parties have lived together in a shared household and are related by consanguinity, marriage, adoption in addition to relationship with family members living together as a joint family[227].

However, whereas the bill enables the wife to file a complaint under the proposed enactment against any relative of the husband or the male partner, it does not enable female

[225] 'Domestic Violence' *http://www.measuredhs.com/pubs/pdf/ FRIND3/15Chapter15.pdf*

[226] *http://sify.com/news/anti-domestic-violence-bill-introduced-in-Kashmir-assembly-news-national-kd0u4ceihga.html* accessed on 4 may 2010

[227] ibid

relatives of the husband or the male partner to file a complaint against the wife or the female partner.[228]

The bill also provides for the right of women to secure housing and to reside in her matrimonial home or shared household, whether or not she has any title or rights there[229].

---

228   Ibid
229   Ibid

CHAPTER III

WOMEN AND ARMED CONFLICT IN KASHMIR

Recent years have seen a resurgence of violence all over the world. While scholars disagree over its reasons, it is generally agreed that the major victims of violence happen to be the excluded and marginalized social groups, in particular, women. Feminist scholarship has recently attempted to unravel, in several excellent studies, the experiences of women affected by ethnic, secessionist, communal and community oriented conflict. Urvashi Batalia and Ritu Menon have, for example, brought to light the pain and sufferings of women affected by the violence following the partition of India.[230] Similarly, Julie Peteet, Lila Abu Lughod

---

[230] See for example ; Menon Ritu and Bhasin Kamla, *Borders and Boundaries: Women in India's Partition*. New Delhi: Kali For Women. 1998.

and others have studied the impact of violence on women in west Asia, in particular, Lebanon, Iraq and Palestine.[231]

If the data provided by Uppsala University, under its 'conflict data program', is to be trusted, about one-sixth of India's citizens live in areas of armed conflict[232]. The Upsala university conflict data program defines armed conflict in the following words:

"An armed conflict is a contested incompatibility that concerns government and/or territory where the use of armed force between two parties, of which at least one is the government of a state, results in at least 25 battle-related deaths in one calendar year"[233].

Kashmir has been described as the most militarized corner in the world due to the presence of more than half a million troops. Since 1989 there has been an active militant insurgency backed by a popular sentiment of '*Azadi*' in Kashmir. According to a Human Rights Report compiled in 2005, there were in the valley 35 lacs troops posted in the valley, whereas the population there was about 57 lacs. In other words, there was a soldier against five to seven civilians. Since 1995 Indian armed forces have armed and trained local auxiliary forces made up of surrendered or captured militants

---

[231] See for example; Therese Saliba, Carolyn Allen, and Judith A. Howard, *Gender, Politics and Islam,* Orient Longman Private Limited, New Delhi, India, 2005

[232] Uppsala university, conflict data program available at *http:// www.pcr.uu.se/research/UCDP/links-faq/faq.html* accessed on November, 10, 2009

[233] Chenoy Anuradha and Kamal.A.Mitra Chenoy (ed.), *Maoist and Other Armed Conflict*, Penguin Books, India, 2010, p.9

to assist in counter insurgency operations. These forces do not wear uniforms and operate outside the normal command structure of the Indian Army and other armed forces. Nevertheless they are considered agents under international law. They are generally referred to as renegades or third force. The Indian army, and its local agents, have committed, and sponsored/supported widespread human rights violation in Kashmir[234].

The root causes of separatism, according to Chenoy and Chenoy, are not only economic, but are a complex mix of denial of rights, injustice, violence and human rights violations[235]. In her view the reality and perception of denial of rights and justice leads to a sense of collective victimhood and narratives of oppression identified with a community. This collective victimization heightens identity consciousness. It also, as she holds, leads to an alienation from the state in larger 'national community'[236]. There have been periods when violence did declined sharply in the valley, as people suffered from conflict fatigue, but these were intermittent events, and have always led to renewed cycles of violence[237].

---

[234] *State of Human Rights in Jammu and Kashmir 1990-2005;* Compiled and collated by Public Commission on Human Rights, published by Parvez Imroz on behalf of Coalition of Civil Society, Srinagar, Hindustan Printers, Shahdara Delhi, 2005, p.1, also see, e.g; Kazi Seema, *Between Democracy and Nation-Gender and Militarization in Kashmir,* Women Unlimited, New Delhi, 2009

[235] Chenoy and Chenoy (ed.), *Maoist and Other Armed conflict,* p. 65

[236] Ibid., p.66

[237] Ibid., P.-52

Increasing evidence show that women experience conflict in a different way to men, something that is confirmed by those working in the field. Almost every instance of an armed conflict undoubtedly affects the entire society, but not to the same measure. Since women are particularly vulnerable, they tend to suffer more than men in almost every instance of armed conflict. War exacerbates the inequalities that exist in different forms and to varying degrees in all societies[238]. Unfortunately, Kashmir has seen a lot of violence in recent years,[239] and while it continues to affect all the people of Kashmir, women bear the scars of violence deeper than men. While scholars have been trying to understand the nature of violence in strife-torn Kashmir, they have made very little effort to unravel the impact of violence on women. My work makes a small effort in that direction, and seeks to reveal how the incessant and ever-increasing violence in Kashmir has changed the lives of women forever. It also makes an effort to draw out the experiences of the female victims of violence in the state—their pain, sorrows and sufferings.

One reason why women are the 'prime targets' in instances of violent conflict is that they are viewed as markers of community identities, and in targeting women, the perpetrators, actually target the community as a whole, its honour, its symbols and prestige. In Kashmir, the media and the human rights bodies have brought to light instances of large scale molestation and rape of women by both the security forces and the militants. There have also been

---

[238] Walikhana charu, *Women Silent Victims In Armed Conflict; An Area Study of Jammu And Kashmir*, Serial Publications, 2004, p.2

[239] Over 9,994 women have been raped and molested, and 22,755 women widowed, cited from *www.kmsnew.org*

instances where the family and/community have 'eliminated' women who had been molested in the armed conflict. For women, therefore, it is not just the state and the militants, but also the community and members of the family who are potential perpetrators of violence against them. Besides rape and molestation, instances have come to light where women were faced with enforced prostitution, sexual slavery and impregnation or termination of pregnancy without, of course, the protection of the rule of law. In almost all such instances, the state has been a mute spectator, failing to provide any sense of protection to women.[240]

Where women are not direct victims of violence, they are still affected by it, nonetheless. Violent conflict in Kashmir have led to the destruction of many homes, and for many women, the loss of the bread earner in their families. Kashmir has seen, since the resurgence of violence, a proliferation of female headed households. Owing to deaths in the conflict but also occasionally as a result of desertion and abandonment by men, the number of female headed household is regularly increasing in Kashmir. Forced by circumstances, these women are thrust into new responsibilities, and are forced to sell their labour to sustain their children.[241] The resurgence of violence in the last several decades has turned many married women into widows and, worse still, half-widows.

---

[240] Walikhana Charu, *Women Silent Victims,*. p.2
[241] Ibid, p.12

Violence on the body of women

The modern state is a gendered state. The processes, values and institutions associated with its construction are gendered as well. In the construction of the nation, women are looked upon as the biological and cultural reproducers of the nation[242]. Kumkum Sangari points out that everyday gendered violence serves to reinforce all other forms of violence in our society, and is a connective tissue between patriarchal systems and social structures, the node at which the social inequalities represented by each of these dominant agencies meet and interact. [243]

As in other conflict ridden societies like Nagaland, Manipur, in Kashmir as well, ethnic identity is tied to the body of women. Since the honour of the community is tied to women, in inter-community violence, women become the primary targets. Often they are targets of violence by members of their own community, and male members of the community target them to maintain the honour of their communities.[244] The most predictable form of violence experienced by women, as women, is when the

---

[242] Amena Mohsin, Silence and Marginality: Gendered Security and The Nation State, IN, F.Fazal, S.Rajagopalan (ed.) *Women, Security, South Asia; A clearing in the Thicket,* Sage Publication, New Delhi, London, 2005 p. 134-136

[243] Sangari Kumkum, Marking time: The Gendered Present and the Nuclear Future, IN, *Nivedini Journal of Gender Studies,* Volume 13, October November 2007, p.-54.

[244] Chenoy Anuradha, M.,'Resources or symbols? Women and Armed conflict in India', IN, Ava Darshan Shrestha and Rita Thapa (ed.), *The Impact of Armed Conflict on Women in South Asia,* Manohar, 2007, p.183

women of one community are sexually assaulted by the men of the other, in an overt assertion of their identity and a simultaneous humiliation of the other by 'dishonouring' their women[245]. Women are raped and abused by other men when they want to 'dishonour' the entire community or as is often asserted in such conflict, to teach them a lesson. Thus according to Anuradha Chenoy women's bodies determine their symbolic value (for their community) and undermine their roles[246]. Women also become victims of genocide under the assumption that violence against women's bodies is symbolically representative of shaming and dishonouring the community, as a whole.[247] In a feminist analysis of the political economy of rape, Rita Manchanda, relates Violence against women with sexual control and the allocation of resources, that is, as an aspect of political and economic violence. Patriarchal societies regard women as their property and consider women's productive and reproductive labour as crucial resource. Abduction and rape become strategies for stripping women of their personal assets and of their political assets-honour or in-particular community honour[248]. More importantly, molestation of women is symbolically read in

---

[245] Kamla Bhasin and Ritu Menon(for India), Nighat Said Khan(for Pakistan) (ed.) *Against All Odds; Essays on Women, Religion and Development from India and Pakistan,* Kali for women, India, 1996, p. 41

[246] Ibid; p.183

[247] Ava Darshan Shrestha and Rita Thapa(ed..), *The Impact of Armed Conflict in South Asia,* Manohar, 2007, p.180

[248] Manchanda Rita, Women's Agency in peace building,: Gender Relations in Post-Conflict Construction, *Economic and Political Weekly (EPW),* Vol. 40, No.44/45, (Oct 29-Nov 4) 2005, p.4737

situations of armed conflict as injuring the community and dishonouring its male members.

Rita Manchanda rightly points out that rape and sexual assault of women in situations of conflict is neither incidental nor private[249]. In a 1995 report to the United Nations Human Rights Commission, the Special Rapporteur on Violence against Women noted that in situations of armed conflict 'rape is the symbolic rape of the community, the destruction of the fundamental elements of a society and culture-the ultimate humiliation of the male enemy'.[250]

It is a known fact that in the present, decades old conflict, in Kashmir, both the both security forces and armed militants have systematically used rape as a weapon to punish, intimidate, coerce, humiliate or degrade their enemies.[251] During 1990's rape by Indian Security forces often occurred during crackdowns, cordon-and search operations which were followed by forcing the civilians to suffer collective punishments in which the security forces assaulted residents, destroyed their homes and raped/molested their women.[252] According to Swarna Rajagopalan, in recent years, wherever security forces have been deployed in south Asia, one has heard stories of soldiers raping local women. Regardless of the veracity of every charge, and the issue as to which party to the conflict is more blameworthy, what matters is that

[249] Manchanda, Rita 'Guns and *Burqa*: Women in the *Kashmir*i Conflict', in Manchanda (ed.) *Women, War and Peace in South Asia; Beyond Victimhood to Agency*), Sage Publications, New Delhi, 2001 p. 72

[250] Walikhana Charu, *Women silent Victims,* p. 1

[251] Manchanda Rita, 'Guns and *Burqa*', p., 73

[252] Walikhana Charu, *Women Silent Victims,* p. 103

such abuse appears to be accepted as part of the war.[253] A study done by Medicins frontiers in Mid-2005 reveal that Kashmiri Women are among the worst sufferers of sexual violence in the world. It further mentions that since the beginning of the armed struggle in Kashmir in 1989, sexual violence has been routinely perpetuated on Kashmiri women, with 11.6 per cent of respondents saying they were victims of sexual abuse.[254]

It is quite difficult to get sufficient data on violence intended on women's bodies, and that too in a conflict situation. Women are often silent victims and suffer violence with muted silence. Women, who dare to speak about the sufferings of their bodies, 'pollute' the communities which in-turn ostracises them. In most cases, of sexual assault which go unnoticed and few cases which get noticed are the ones in which it is still not the raped women themselves, but their menfolk who do the talking. They highlight these incidents of rape and/or molestation to de-legitimate the state, and to project it as an aggressor, rather than a protector to civilians that it ought to be. Anuradha distinguishes raped women into two categories. One category of raped women get shunned, while the other end up becoming symbols in the conflict. Just as the militants highlight incidents where the security forces are involved, the state points to cases of rape and molestation of women where the finger of accusation is pointed and against the militants. The state highlights the

---

253 Rajagopalan Swarna 'Women and Security: in Search of a New Paradigm' IN Faizal Sarah and Swarna,(ed;) *Women, Security South Asia,* p.60

254 Saeed-ur-Rehman Siddiqui, '*Women day in Kashmir*' Wailing *Woes,* http://www.*Kashmir*newz.com/a0027.html accesses on 12 April 2010

atrocities committed by the militants in an attempt to isolate them. A report[255] released by the army in Srinagar states; that the women of the state have been constantly subjected to the brutalities of the militants.[256] The sexual appropriation of Kashmiri Muslim women by the military functions not just as an especially potent political weapon, but also a cultural weapon to inflict collective humiliation on Muslim Kashmiri men.[257] In Kashmir both security forces and armed militants have systematically used rape as a weapon to punish, intimidate, coerce, humiliate or degrade the common people.[258] Both pundit and Muslim women were sexually targeted by the militants There are several incidents where both the militants and the security forces have raped women to punish the men in their families for their suspect loyalties·

According to a report prepared by Jammu Kashmir Coalition of Civil Societies (JKCCS), rape has been routinely used as a war weapon in Kashmir (See fig. 3.1 and 3.2). Documented cases have shown evidence of mass rape during

---

[255] *Indian Army, Human Rights Violations and Atrocities by Terorrists,* Cited from Chenoy Anuradha, 'Resources or Symbols?' p. 190

[256] Chenoy Anuradha, 'Resources or Symbols?' p. 190-191

[257] Kazi Seema, *Gender and Militarization,* p. 155.

[258] Manchanda Rita, 'Guns and *Burqa*', p. 72, 73

Fig 3.1 Rapes/Molestations from 1990 to Aug 2005 (Agency)

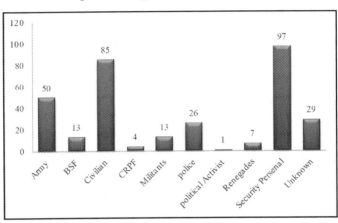

Fig 3.2 Rapes/Gang Rapes and Molestations from 1990 to August 2005

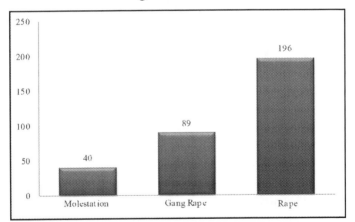

Source: *The state of Human Rights in Jammu and* Kashmir, *1990-2005*

cordon and search operations by security forces. There have also come to light several cases of abduction of women and their subsequent rape within Army facilities and a complete disregard for age, health and disability in the perpetuation of sexual violence. Mass rape of Kashmiri women by the security forces was first documented in the Chanapora (Srinagar) mass rape incident on in March 1990[259]. This was followed by another grave incident in Kunan Poshpora which allegedly witnessed the mass rape of women during a cordon—and—search operation in February 1991[260]. It is alleged that the troops raped the village women all though the night. Eleven year old girls, pregnant women, to 60 year old grandmother were raped. In raping them the security forces were punishing and humiliating the entire community[261]. In 1996 in Bomai Sopore, in, when the people were holding protest demonstrations against the excesses of army personnel, several girls were dragged to paddy fields where the security men open their garments, bruised their faces and raped them.[262] There are several

---

[259] Ibid p. 73

[260] During a cordon—and—search operation by the 4th Rajputana Rifles of 68 Mountain Brigade on the night of 23 and 24 Feberuary 1991, there was a crackdown in the entire by the troops of Rajputana Rifles. There had been heavy snowfall the earlier night and the troops asked all the men of the village to come out of their homes. They gathered at Kunan Chowk for interrogation leaving the women and children alone at their homes.

[261] Cf. Manchanda, 'Guns and *Burqa*'; p. 73-74, Also see *State of Human Rights in Jammu and Kashmir 1990-2005,* p. 274,

[262] *Rape and Molestation; A weapon of war in Kashmir*(A consolidated report on various Atrocities committed on women folk in *Kashmir* under the national conference government;) prepared by: The Jammu and *Kashmir* Human

incidents where the security forces entered houses, one after the other and sexually assaulted women.[263] In one village, reportedly there were complaints of Army Personnel stripping themselves in front of womenfolk of the village.[264]

In looking at why women become special targets in a situation of war it seems that rape as a war weapon has been often used to punish the civilians following any militant attack. Women in such attacks have been chosen randomly. For instance in 1993 a large number of women were raped during a search operation after a peaceful demonstration against Hazratbal siege was fired upon in Bijbehara in Anantnag and over 60 people were killed.[265] Thus women often become the targets like other civilians assaulted or killed, simply because they happen to be in the wrong place at the wrong time.[266] Rape has been used as a means of targeting women whom the security forces accuse of being militant sympathizers; in raping them the security forces were attempting to punish and humiliate the entire community. This is exemplified by an incident (among many) in which two sisters of a militant were raped by the Rashtriya Rifles, men of the Indian army in 1997 at village Hakura in District Anantnag[267]. In 2005, the BSF troops

---

Rights Awareness and Documentation Centre, Srinagar, No. 32, Institute of *Kashmir* Studies, Srinagar, March 1998, p.2

[263] Ibid p. 13

[264] *Jammu State of Human Rights in Jammu and Kashmir 1990-2005*; p.28

[265] Ritu Dewan, 'Humsheera', Humsaya: Sisters, Neighbours, Women's Testimonies From *Kashmir, Economic and Political Weekly,* Oct-8 1994, p. 2655

[266] Walikhana Charu, *Women Silent Victims.*, p. 104

[267] *Rape and Molestation; A Weapon of War in Kashmir*, 1998, p.3

raided the house of one Abdul Jabbar Malik of Vailu Village in Kokernag, Anantnag and raped his two sisters.[268]

Cases have been documented where a group of soldiers allegedly molested women, refusing to spare even the ones who were pregnant. In one case study, by Independent Women' initiative for Justice (IWIJ)[269], Uma Chakarborty, has rightly pointed out that the graph of rapes in Kashmir compared to other Right abuses is very low, but this is because most of the rape cases are not reported by the victims and their families. The victims do not come forward in most of the cases because of the social stigma attached to a rape victim. Besides, most of the rapes occur in remote areas which have little access to media or the human rights groups[270]. Crimes against women in Kashmir exist in many other forms too. One such crime is the shameful sexual harassment often verbal harassment and molestation which erodes any sense of security for women in the valley. Kashmiri women are often subjected to humiliating body searches by the security men. Kashmiri women, on way to their college or office, are often subjected to body searches. This is what happens to a well-off, educated woman in Kashmir, needless to say that poorer women's sufferings are much dreadful[271]. In order to enquire on the matter, I asked

---

[268] *Voices Unheard*, Srinagar, Vol- 10, April-June 2005.

[269] IWIJ comprised of women (lawyers, law researchers, a medical doctor, journalist, and women's rights activists.

[270] Shopian: Manufacturing a Suitable Story; A Case Watch, Independent Women's initiative for Justice Shopian 2009 *http://kafilabackup.files.wordpress.com/2009/12/iwij-report-shopian-10-dec-2009.pdf*, Downloaded from www. *Kashmir*times.com accessed on 15th October 2011

[271] Rajagopalan Swarna, 'Women and Security', P.60

my respondents if they were ever sexually harassed by the armed forces and 41% of my respondents replied in the positive (See fig 3.3). One woman from Anantnag District told me that, she stopped working in the agricultural fields, because the armed forces were continually harassing her with verbal abuses. This Woman was above 45 years of age and one could easily guess how difficult it must be for the younger women to venture out.

In a conflict zone like Kashmir, this direct assault on Women is one way of attacking the masculinity of the community and their sense of honor and prestige. It is this that often prompts the victims to take their own lives, before their 'enemies' succeed in 'polluting' their bodies. In one such case, Zahida, from Changoo, Doru Shahabad, took her life with a sharp knife when an army official entered her house to molest her, on being unsuccessful, he allegedly opened fire and pumped bullets in her abdomen. Her close relatives revealed that on realizing the intensions of the armed person, she had actually killed herself (See Appendix IIIA).

Fig 3.3   Harassment by the Security Forces

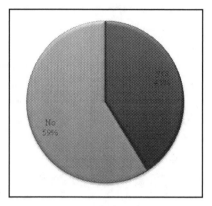

Source: Field Survey by the Researcher

Women who suffer gender violence have always experienced the bitter process of 'othering' by both sides.[272] In some cases, militants have raped women whose family members were believed to be informers or supporters of rival groups. A 16 year old girl daughter of a (Central Reserved Police Force) CRPF Jawan was allegedly gang raped by militants, the reason being her father's job.[273] During 1990's when the militancy was on peak, militants and Armed Forces were both using women as informers. The abduction of women and forced marriages is common throughout the militancy affected areas of Jammu and Kashmir, especially at the hands of militants who have surrendered and enjoy the patronage

---

[272]   Bhasin Anuradha Jamwal, Women in Kashmir Conflict: Victimhood and Beyond, IN, Shree Mulay and Jackie Kirk (ed.) *Women Building Peace Between India and Pakistan,* Anthem Press, India, 2007, P. 103,104

[273]   *State of Human Rights in Jammu and Kashmir 1990-2005.,* p.35

of security forces. In most cases, the arrest of these women does not mean rescue for them, it means being engaged by the other side for the same tasks[274].

In recent years many cases have come to light where women have been pressurized by the army or unidentified gunmen to work with them as informers. Two girls from Budgam, named Zaheeda and Nuzhat were shot at. First, the girls were dubbed as militant aides and then forced by the security personnel to work for them and when they refused, they were shot dead.[275] The incidence of women working for army and militants has shown some resurgence in the recent times. One Dilshada Bano was mysteriously shot dead by unidentified gunmen in June 2004. Her husband had disappeared in custody and she was contesting the case in State Human Rights Commission (SHRC) and was a member of APDP. People in her native village said that she was an informer and that is why she was killed by the militants[276]. The present conflict has seen a considerable loss of male members and it is left to women to follow the cases of ex-gratia and SRO-43 (See Appendix—IIIB). These women have to visit various security camps to ascertain death of the killed or whereabouts of disappeared. Often the army personnel take undue advantage and make them do regular rounds and sometimes force them to work

---

[274] Bhasin Anuradha Jamwal,' Women in *Kashmir* Conflict' p. 103

[275] The army on the pretext of having links with militants arrested Sakina from Bandipora. The Army even claimed recovery of weapons from her possession, a claim which was strongly refuted by police.cited from, State of Human Rights in Human rights in Jammu and *Kashmir*.

[276] *State of Human Rights in Human Rights in Jammu and Kashmir 1990-2005*; p. 278

for them. Even in the regular offices here women pursue their cases they have to face humiliation from lower to higher ups in bureaucracy[277]. Many women have been forced by armed forces to work as informers and in case of refusal have been booked under PSA (See Appendix—IIIC and IIID)· Official statistics record that 11 girls were abducted and murdered after 1993, 35 in 1994 and for the first half of 1995, there were 3 abductions of girls and women.[278] According to an estimate of JKCCS, there were 225, rape/molestation cases in Kashmir inflicted by the armed forces (See Fig 3.2 and 3.3) from 1990 till August 2005.[279]

In determining when to bring indictments for rape and sexual assault in armed conflict, the prosecution in the court to take account of the rules of Evidence and procedure and the adequacy and reliability of available evidence, Investigations of crimes against women in Rwanda have raised the numerous practical and legal problems, which are equally applicable in the conflict situation in Jammu and Kashmir: these are

i) The dispersal of victims and witnesses across regions of the world;

ii) The unwillingness of women to speak of crimes committed against them through humiliation, shame, fear of public or family ostracism or fear of reprisal

---

[277] Ibid.

[278] UNI Report in the *Times of India*, 24 Nov 1995.), also see ; Manchanda Rita, 'Guns and *Burqa*', P. 81

[279] Walikhanna Charu, *Women Silent Victims,.*, p.103

iii) The intervention of too many people wanting accounts of their experiences, including media, NGOs, support agencies etc, and eventually official investigators;[280]

iv) The passage of time and the desire not to relive such atrocities; and the feeling that rape and sexual assault were not in fact of major concern compared with the loss of community, home and possessions and the death or disappearance of family members.[281]

Until recently, incidents of rape in Kashmir had largely escaped international scrutiny and condemnation, including allegedly committed by the armed forces. In the past, rape was often accepted as 'spoils of war' or mischaracterized as incidental to the conflict or as privately motivated form of sexual abuse rather than an abuse of power that implicates public responsibility. Reports of the widespread use of rape as a tactic of war in the former Yogoslavia have been instrumental in focusing attention on the function of rape in armed conflict and have provoked international condemnation. Such condemnation needs to extended to the use of rape in internal conflict as well.[282]

The unfortunate part of violence on women is that their bodies become the markers of identity. Their individuality is curbed and their sufferings become a means of publicising their positive victimhood. The victimhood of women is publicised and politicised, to fulfil the political objectives of

---

[280] Christine Chinklin, 'Amicus Curae Brief on Proctective Measures for victims and witnesses' (1996) 7 *Criminal Law Forum*, p.179,185 cited from Ibid

[281] Walikhana Charu; *Women Silent Victims.*, p. 106

[282] *State of Human Rights in Jammu and Kashmir* 1990-2005, p. 276

both the state and the militants. The rape of Kashmiri women by the security forces was viewed as an integral political event in the people's struggle but the political leadership in publicly projecting rape as a war crime, failed at the same time, to politically challenge the patriarchal code within which women's victimhood serves to deny agency to women[283].

State, militants and Women

Armed conflict is a typically masculine activity, marked by violence, aggression and force. There are indeed certain deep rooted social and political grievances that legitimate these conflict, but the violence and force on which they depend to realise their objectives cause untold pain and suffering for ordinary men and women. An important feature of armed conflict is that it operates within a masculinist frame of reference, and sets out hierarchical roles and attributes for men and women in their respective societies[284]. Scholarly work has shown that most of the actors involved in a conflict are men, and even when women form a significant part of the structure of the insurgent/militant group, their military and organizational roles are unlikely to be as significant as those of men. It is the ordinary people, women in particular, who suffer the most in these conflict. Women often find themselves caught between the warring factions and face the consequences of social fragmentation and disruption of homes, social networks and livelihoods[285].

---

[283]   Manchanda Rita, 'Guns and *Burqa*'; p.75
[284]   Chenoy and .Chenoy,(ed.) *Maoist and other Armed Conflict*, p.180
[285]   Ava and Rita (ed.)., *The Impact of Armed Conflict*, p.15

It is interesting to note that to define the Kashmir as a Nation Sheikh Abdullah appropriated the fourteenth century historical Symbol of Kashmir*iyat*, a secular ethnic concept (on which Kashmir was to be based), expounded by the Kashmiri ruler 'Zain-ul-Abideen', and popularised by a woman called 'Lal-Ded'[286], The notion of *Kasmiriyat* transcended religious divisions, and was an regional identity that included both the Muslims and the Hindus living in Kashmir.[287] At the same time, the notion of Kashmir*iyat* that has so insistently been invoked by the secessionists, insurgents, militants and the mainstream political parties in Kashmir has worked to marginalise women by presenting them as its bearer, and symbolic representatives. Since women have come to be seen as bearers of Kashmir*iyat*, the community, in particular the men in the community, have appropriated the right to discipline and control them, and if necessary, with violent means. Women in Kashmir have often been targets of community and family-induced violence, perpetrated on their bodies in the interest of the need to preserve the regional Kashmiri identity.

In Kashmir there was little proof of women combatants in militant organisations, until some of them were arrested by the army. This indicates that some women militants were, and are still, a part of the underground militant

---

[286] A mystic Hindu Women, revered by both Muslims and Hindus equally.

[287] Reeta Chowdhari Tremblay, 'Identity and Nationalism: Where are Women *in Kashmiri Politics?*'; IN Shree mulay and Jakie Kirk (ed.) *Speaking Cross Borders*: *Women Building Peace Between India and Pakistan*, Antham Press: Delhi, Publishing Company, Delhi, 2007

organisations[288] . While in Nagaland and Manipur, women cadres are present in significant numbers in the insurgent and national liberation groups, in Kashmir, on the other hand, some women's organisations defending extremist positions exist, but women are not represented in the more important political organisations of the militants[289]. Women become activists and support peace processes in different ways during conflict, from their homes, rather informally through community interaction and as active negotiators. In Kashmir like in NE, women have supported struggles in their daily chores, by bearing the burden of missing men, by their songs and stories that they pass on to children and by their caring roles. As Anuradha puts it, 'Women do not have to be in the public sphere to be activists, since politics enters the private domain especially during conflict. Their very struggle to survive, fend for their families, and eke out a living requires tactics and strategies no less than those on the war front'[290]. Women's involvement in armed conflict can be strategic, circumstantial, or by choice. Very often, women relatives of militants and security forces have no choice but to be a part of the 'infra-structure' in conflict situations.

Women militants in the valley have largely confined themselves to secondary roles, like nursing and care-giving, the support they render to insurgent forces is more or less social and cultural in nature. At the same time, they do not take up leadership roles, and are not likely to have any presence or representation in the peace talks as and when they are held.[291]

---

[288] Anuradha M.Chenoy 'Resources or Symbols?', p. 197
[289] Ibid, p. 194
[290] Ibid p. 198
[291] Ibid p. 198

Women increasingly play multiple roles, as combatants, protesters and peacemakers, but they are valued less than men. Women do not have key roles in decision making structures and leadership of the state or amongst insurgent groups. Societies perceive women primarily in gender—stereotyped roles and this image gets reinforced in situations of armed conflict and insurgency strengthened[292]. Anjum Zamruda Habib serves a typical example of such a case. She was one of the founding members of Hurriyat Conference. She was the chairperson of Muslim Khwateen Markaz,—the women's wing of Hurriyat conference. In 2003 she was arrested in Delhi and convicted under the Prevention of terrorism Act (POTA). Anjum in her prison dairy which was later published in the form of a book by Sahiba Hasan, says that she was a member of *All Party Hurriyat Conference* (APHC) and had connections with the well known Hurriyat leaders. Anjum in her book recapitulates that Rita Manchanda and Tapan Bose had brought the *Wakalatnama*-power of attorney to her but she didn't sign it in the hope that APHC would arrange a lawyer for her[293]. But as she points out, when she got arrested none among these leaders gave her any importance, and assist her. They tried their best and to a large extent succeeded in getting their male co-associates released. The worst was that her name was not included in the list of names of Kashmiri prisoners submitted by the APHC to the Government of India with a recommendation that they be released.[294] They had abandoned her although she was an active member and

---

[292]   Chenoy and Chenoy, *Women and Other Armed Conflict,* p.180

[293]   Anjum Zamruda Habib, *Prisoner No. 100, My Life In An Indian Prison,* tr. by Sahiba Hussain, Zubaan, New Delhi,2011 p.13

[294]   Ibid., p. 42

associate of Hurriyat. Anjum Zamruda's feels that she was discriminated by the separatist leaders only because she was a woman. As she puts it;

> *I personally believe that perhaps they did not wish to encourage woman's leadership role or maybe they simply lacked the basic courtesy to enquire after me or look into whether or not I needed legal assistance. Could it be just a coincidence that they made every possible effort to get our male colleague released but left me to rot in jail?* [295]. *According to her account, her family members had met the then chairperson of Hurriyat. They told her mother zamrud is a very brave woman. She will endure the hardship and it will not take more than five years'. Zamruda blames it be 'a game' of her entry to the jail that was already fixed for five years* [296].

In her early works, Manchanda presents two narratives about women in the Kashmir conflict. The first derives from a human rights discourse where women figure as victims of direct (state) and indirect violence that transforms them into widows and half-widows of the disappeared or bereaved mothers of lost sons and children. The second centres on the *Kashmiriyat* on the conventional patriarchal ideology of Kashmiri struggle in which woman symbolise the grieving mother, the martyr's mother and the raped

---

[295]   Ibid p. 22
[296]   Ibid p. 173

women.[297] The representation of Kashmiri women as victims rather than survivors does not correspond with Women's subjective experience and removes them from the political canvas of militarization. However scholars who have worked in Palestine and Algeria, hold that, are the iconic representations of the nation, in a nationalist movement. In protracted military conflict with its attendant loss of life, women, in particular the mother of the martyr, symbolise life giving or national generativity, loss and sacrifice[298].

According to the scholars working in other conflict ridden societies, Women reshape their homes as war fronts, and even as mothers and housewives get informally affiliated with resistance movement.[299] Kashmiri women have also seemingly chosen to blend the home and the front to nourish political activism. At local weddings, women were eager to have a resistance fighter or *Mujahid* in their festivities. They would break out into a *Wanuwan*, the traditional Kashmiri song of celebration, intertwining couplets in praise of local *Mujahids*. Mothers, sisters and aunts would bask the glory of a *Mujahid* relative who had gone across for training[300].

In the mass protests 2008-2010 an increasing number of women participated alongside men: at times even leading all-women protest marches. Interestingly women engaged

---

[297] Manchanda, Rita 'Guns and *Burqa:*' p.; 43

[298] Julie Peteet, 'Icons and Militants: Mothering in the Danger Zone', IN, Therese, Carolyn, Allen,(ed.) *Gender, Politics and Islam*, p.139

[299] Ibid p. 141,142

[300] Manchanda Rita (ed.)., 'Guns and *Burqa*', P.51

in stone-throwing; together with chanting anti-India and pro-freedom slogans.[301]

These women get classified as combatants by sheer location. Women relatives supported, gave shelter to the militants and played active roles in the militancy. They suffered severe consequences if the police/army discovered their linkages to extremists[302]. Women relatives of state officials like police and army wives have been termed by analysts as the forgotten and invisible 'other', which have to grapple with trauma, widowhood and tragedy and have generally been ignored by Human rights activists of the region and by the state[303]. State and society treat relatives of victims in different ways, depending on their status[304]. Thus it seems that apart from social patriarchy women in Kashmir are the victims of militaristic patriarchy as well.

One cannot dismiss the 'disappearance' of women as stray events, since, in many cases, women have been recovered from the hide-outs of militants. No reports of women being picked up have been lodged by families, most likely out of fear that such a step brings greater shame and indignity[305].

---

[301] *http://english.aljazeeranet/indepth/spotlight/ Kashmirtheforgottenconflict/2011/07/201173/9958721770.html.*

[302] Chenoy Anuradha, 'Resources or Symbols?' p.187

[303] Roshni Goswami, *Reinforcing subordination, an analysis of women in armed conflict situations* *www.isiswomen.org/wia/ wia399/pea00001.html*

[304] Chenoy Anuradha, 'Resources or Symbols' p.187

[305] Anurahda Bhasin Jamwal, 'Women in *Kashmir* Conflict', p.106

It is obvious that women from militant families become by the security forces particular targets of harassment[306]. They suffer intimidation by the security forces even after the suspected militants had been eliminated. Sometimes they have to suffer for their close male relative's decision to become a Militant[307]. They face routine questioning and harassment from the security forces. They also suffer from social isolation. Based on various testimonies, several studies have shown that there is very little social acceptance for the militants, and particularly after 1995, people don't want to be seen associating with militant families[308]. In the initial years of militancy, women in Kashmir valley were in the forefront, protesting against custodial killings or torture of youths at the hands of security forces. There was a conspicuous silence in cases of rape, but when it came to custodial killings or disappearances. There were vocal protests by both men and women, Women deliberately positioned themselves as a shield for men-folk and remained at the forefront, through a voluntary decision at such protest demonstration[309]. The political leadership has often involved religion to ensure the support of women to their side, presenting their dead sons and husbands as glorious

---

[306] Walikhana in her book, *Women Silent Victims* narrates, 'Jana's son, Fayaz Ahmad Dar, was a member of the hizbul mujahideen. She hasn't seen him since long, but the, security forces constantly question her about his whereabouts. Twice they have set her house in warpora village on fire. Desperately poor, jana's is a lonely battle for daily survival. Her neighbours avoid her'.

[307] Ramachandran Sudha, *The Shades of Violence; Women and Kashmir,* WISCOMP, New Delhi 2003, p.18

[308] Ibid

[309] Bhasin Anurdaha Jamwal, 'Women in *Kashmir* Conflict' P.106

martyrs[310]. After the Amarnath Shrine Board agitation, JKLF chairman—Yasin Malik handed out *Shahid Maqbool Butt* award to the mothers of those young boys who were killed in the agitation in Srinagar in 2008. The mothers were reported to have said that they were guaranteed a good place in heaven so there was no problem in giving up their sons. They would meet them again in heaven[311].

In ethnic and nationalist struggles, the glorification of women as biological regenerators of the nation, combined with a complete disregard for them as people results in massive abuse of their reproductive rights and maternal emotions. This has happened in Kashmir too. In early 1990's militant groups imposed a ban on the use of contraceptives and on abortions. People, especially in the villages were told that the central government was trying to alter the Muslim majority nature of the state and so Muslims should have more children and besides, the armed conflict needed more fighters. The sale of contraceptives was stopped and family planning procedures were not performed at least openly. The role of women was to ensure a continuous supply of fighters. Mothers were exhorted to send their sons to fight. Those who did were praised as 'patriotic mothers'. Mothers were told not to grieve for sacrificing their sons in order to motivate others to sacrifice.[312] To motivate women for

---

[310] Ava, Rita(ed.), *The impact of Armed Conflict,* p.18

[311] Parashar Swati, Gender, Jihad, and Jingoism : Women as Perpetrators, Planners, and Patrons of Militancy in *Kashmir, Studies in Conflict Terrorism, Volume: 34, Issue: 4,* TAYLOR &FRANCIS, 2011, p.310

[312] Ramachandran Sudha, *The Shades of Violence'* P.21-22 ; One Khatija bi did not stop her son from joining the armed struggle. When her son died, khatijah was praised for the

sacrificing their male relatives they were preached '*shaheed ki jo maut hai wo quam ki hayat hai*'—he who dies a martyr, gives life to the nation). Women protected militants hiding in their homes by telling the security forces then that they were their husbands. In ethnic and nationalist struggles, women often serve as couriers of cultural and ideological traditions. Women are expected to dress and behave in ways that are prescribed by tradition[313].

Valentine Mogadham has categorised two kinds of revolutionary movements one ethno-nationalist separatist movements and the other religio-political movements[314]. The first uses women as a symbol of liberation and project women's emancipation as an important revolutionary agenda as in case of separatist movement of Srilanka[315]. The second one uses women as a symbol of the national culture and tradition that are to be reclaimed as in case of Kashmri separatist movements. In this case women are virtually excluded from formal participation. In the case of Kashmir, women have managed to give logistical support to militants and women's groups are unfortunately playing a vital role in enforcing fundamentalist Islamist Ideology in Jammu and Kashmir, where predominantly liberal Sufi form of Islam had thrived for centuries.[316] While this does not indeed hold true

---

sacrifice she had made. They would tell her over and over again not to grieve. And she first believed it. But latter, she started feeling lost and pain

[313]   Ibid p.22

[314]   Cf; Parashar Swati, Feminist IR and Women Militants: Case Studies from South Asia" IN *Cambridge Review of International Affairs*, June 2009, p.240

[315]   Ibid., p. 240

[316]   Ibid., p. 249

for all the groups, the attractions of the hyper-masculinist and puritan Islam for an increasing number of women is a worrying trend in Kashmir.

In Kashmir, it is a regrettable fact that the state is not a protector against, but a perpetuator of, violence against women. Armed with the Armed Forces Special Power Act (See Appendix IIIE), the security forces routinely target ordinary civilians, including, women, free from the constraints set by the laws and the judiciary. Anuradha Bhasin, rightly points out that women are raped and molested by combatant forces in armed conflict as a form of vengeance and control. The state, she further says in such situations devises different acts and strategies to shield the culprits in uniform.[317]

In Kashmir, the state has often been accused of shielding the criminals. In Kunan Poshpora, in 1991, in one incident over 30 women and children were raped by the army. No adequate official enquiry was held. The police refused to file an FIR because they did not want to annoy the army' despite detailed affidavit clearly indicting the army on charges of rape.[318]The army subsequently invited the independent press council of India to investigate the incident. The Press Council agreed to that and appointed a three-member committee, headed by B. G. Verghese[319]. The Verghese Commitee visited the

---

[317] Bhasin Anuradha Jamwal,' Women in *Kashmir* Conflict'; p. 96,97

[318] *State of Human Rights in Jammu and Kashmir 1990-2005* ; p.274

[319] Though it was a three member Committee, it was actually conducted by George Verguese only, and therefore the report came to be known as the Verghese Committee Report..

village more than three months after the incident occurred. After interviewing a number of the alleged victims, the committee concluded that the incident was a trick set up to frame the army. The committee rejected the allegations merely on the ground of inconsistencies in the women's stories and variations in the number of rapes alleged to have taken place.[320] In the final report, they gave a clean chit to the security forces on such frivolous grounds that the girls were found to be giggling when asked if they had been raped.[321]

Even in the cases where it was proved that security forces had raped certain women, they were not prosecuted. In a much publicized case, a young bride was detained and she and her aunt were raped by BSF soldiers while she was travelling to her husband's home. The Indian authorities ordered the police to conduct an enquiry. Although the enquiry concluded that the women had been raped, the security forces were never prosecuted.[322] Instances such as

---

[320]   Rape In *Kashmir*. A Crime of war, *Asia Watch A Division of Human Rights Watch & Physicians for Human Rights* *http://www.hrw.org/sites/default/files/reports/INDIA935.PDF*
It is believed that the committee examined medical reports based on examinations conducted on 32 of the women two to three weeks later, on March 15 and 21, 1991, which confirmed that the hymens of three of the unmarried women had been torn. The committee concluded that the medical evidence was "worthless", that "such a delayed medical examination proves nothing" and that such abrasions are "common among the village folk in *Kashmir*." About the torn hymens, the committee argued that they could be the result of "natural factors, injury or premarital sex.

[321]   Bhasin Anuradha Jamwal, 'Women in *Kashmir* Conflict'; p. 95

[322]   Amnesty International, India; 'Torture, Rape and Deaths in custody', (London; March, 1992)p.21

these are far too many to be recounted here. More recently, owing to initiative of IWIJ (Independent women's initiative for justice) the double Shopian rape case captured the attention of the media, but we must bear in mind that the for Kashmiri women the shameful incident was neither exceptional nor unprecedented. The security forces are viewed by Kashmiri women with considerable fear and apprehension, indeed!

Social effects of violence on women

Since the insurgency in Kashmir, a large number of Women have seen the deaths of their loved ones, and often, the loss of the bread-earner in the family, either a father or a spouse. Every death in the family leads to the destruction of the family, as a viable socio-economic unit. It creates immediate problems of sustenance and emotional security for the family members. Since the responsibility for the maintenance of the household then falls on the hapless women, it creates immense social and psychological problems for them, which most women, in the absence of trained counseling centers, find impossible to cope and handle. This has, as several studies have revealed, led to a dramatic increase in suicides by women in the post-insurgency period.[323]

Military action in Jammu and Kashmir is covered under the Armed forces (Special Powers) Act, 1958 (As Amended in 1972). Under the Act (See Appendix—IIIE), even a Non-Commissioned officer can order his men to shoot

---

[323] Afsana Rashid, Women Suicide Rate in Valley Rising, *Voices Unheard,* July-Sep 2005 p.5-6

to kill if he thinks that it is necessary for maintenance of public order. The Act permits arrest without warrants with whatever force necessary of any person against whom there is an iota of suspicion[324]. The most draconian aspect of the Act is the immunity it offers to the security forces, against prosecution. Unaccountable to the court of law, the armed forces have been responsible for the loss of many lives. The armed militants have similarly killed many Kashmiri's, under one pretext or the other treating these deaths as necessary for the armed struggle. It immediately leads to the destruction of the family as a social unit, and renders women, widows and their children, orphans. It then falls on women to provide livelihoods, and widows are pushed into the labour market, where they are under-paid, and suffer continued exploitation at the hands of their employers. According to one study, the period of insurgency in Kashmir has shown a marked increase in the female labour[325].

In a study by Dabla, it was revealed, that about, one-third of the widows were in the age-group of 31-45[326]. Over half of these women, (53.67%) live alone, and even though remarriage is not forbidden, a mere 8.66 percent remarried. When asked, 89% of widows were against remarriage[327]. Several families were actually found to have no male members left. At least 25 families in Trehgam village are

---

[324] Bhasin Anuradha Jamwal, 'Women in *Kashmir* Conflict' ; p.173

[325] Afsana Rashid, *Waiting for Justice, Half-widows* p.10

[326] Save Chidren Fund to support NGO in rehabilitating Valley Orphans, *Kashmir Times,* May 7, 2000

[327] Dabla Bashir Ahmad, *Widows and Orphans In Kashmir,* JAYKAY Publications, Srinagar, 2010, P. 65

all-women households.[328] Even in case where widows received support from their extended family, it was found to be insufficient to meet both the material and emotional needs of the widows and their children. According to an estimate, in rural Kashmir, widows are reporting on average 3-6 children.[329]

According to a recent report by APDP, titled '*Half-life half-widow*' like most conflict situations, gendered violence in Kashmir has been systemic but typically overshadowed by attention to 'harder' security matters. The report has pointed out that violence against women has prevented accurate assessments of the actual harms preserved by women, for example, due to widowhood[330].

Enforced disappearance is one of the most harrowing consequences of the armed conflict in Kashmir. It has been argued in several scholarly studies that the lower-middle classes were more directly involved in the public mobilisation for *Azadi* and therefore subject to greater repression by the state. The prolonged, often permanent absence of male family members is particularly detrimental for women from weaker socio-economic backgrounds, where the absence of male kin has severe economic implications.[331] During

---

[328] Ramachandran Sudha *The Shades of Violence*', p. 17

[329] Suri Kavita, *Impact of violence on women's education in Kashmir*, WISCOMP, New Delhi, 2006., p. 38,39

[330] Half Widow-Half life, Responding to Gendered Violence in *Kashmir*, A report by Association of parents of disappeared persons, *http://kafilabackup.files.wordpress.com/2011/07/half-widow-half-wife-apdp.report.pdf p.3*

[331] Sarwan Kashani, Idrees kanth and Gowhar Fazili(ed.), *The Impact of Violence on the Student Community in Kashmir*,

the last decade and a Half, thousands of people have been summarily arrested and detained under PSA, TADA, and POTA. The enforced disappearance in the valley has given rise to, what has come to be known as Half-widows,-women whose spouses have neither been declared dead nor have they returned back to their places of residence. Absence of proof of death makes life miserable for the half-widows and they continue to live with uncertain future[332].

According to a report of 2011 there are about 1500 half-widows in the valley.[333] The report took cognizance of the half-widows of civilians, militants as well as 'suspected militant' members who joined APDP and have pursued disappearance cases are wives of civilian. According to the report, 1,417 cases of disappearances documented by the APDP reveal a common pattern. The forces enter and search a house and take a male member with them who is never seen again. In most cases, wives and other family, members who go looking for their loved ones are sent from one military base to another, one jail to another, each suggesting some clue at the next. Usually, there frantic searches end up in vain, and the family returns back empty-handed.[334]. The condition of half-widows is rendered worse owing to the fact that they cannot remarry, unsure of the fate of their spouses, and are denied the paltry state assistance that is offered to the widows[335]. Most of these women—the widows, half widows and the mothers of missing sons, are unemployed and are sustained by relatives,

---

Oxford, India, 2003 p.35

[332] Half-life-Half Widow; *http://kafilabackup.files.wordpress.com/2011/07/half-widow-half-wife-apdp.report.pdf* p.1

[333] Ibid

[334] Ibid

[335] Avita Rita, *Impact of Armed Conflict on Women*, p. 16

neighbours, NGO's, meagre government relief, parents, and their husband's pensions. A few among them eke out their living starting part-time businesses, or by making handicraft goods or by tilling their small fields. Government sanctioned financial support, especially in the case of civilian killings, usually reaches the widows after two or more years of the death of their husbands[336]. According to Dabla's study, 101/300 (33.6%) widows, were provided financial support by Governmental organisations, the relatives provided support to 99/300 widows, and only 7.3 (22/300) widows were provided any financial support by NGO's. [337] One Firdous a resident of, Srinagar was arrested by the army. He was arrested and booked under PSA for two years. Firdous was later asked by the army to work as their informer and on his refusal to do so, he was, presumably 'eliminated' by the army. After his disappearance, his mother, Fatima applied for the ex-gratia relief as well as benefit under SRO-43 of 1994. However, neither the whereabouts of Firdous were revealed nor any relief provided to the family.[338] In another much publicised case of Parveena Akhter v/s state and others petition no. 64/91 case, even the finding of the inquiry conducted by senior additional Sessions judge, Srinagar had observed that the National Security Guard arrested Javaid during the intervening night of 17-18 august 1990 and thereafter he disappeared. It has been almost 2 decades now and the state has neither confirmed his death, nor has it, handed him back to his family.[339]

---

[336] Suri Kavita, *Impact of Violence on education,* p.39

[337] Dabla, Bashir Ahmad, A. *A Sociological Study of Widows and orphans in Kashmir,* P. 70

[338] *Informative Missive,* April 2006 p.5,6

[339] *State of Human Rights in Jammu and Kashmir, 1990-2005,* p.5

The social impact of conflict is most visible in the emergence of women-headed households, Widows or half-widows are abruptly thrust into a position of responsibility owing to the need to sustain the family.[340] According to the official records, the total number of disappeared persons registered by the state is 693. As per the standing rules next of kins of missing persons are entitled to Rs. 1 lakh as ex-gratia relief after fulfilling all codal formalities. Ex-gratia in favour of 332 cases has been sanctioned[341]. Half-widows, generally refrain from demanding any ex-gratia relief and the popular feeling is that they should accept compensation at all. This is owing to two reasons. One because she isn't sure about her husband's death and two, because she would be accepting money from the very state actors who are responsible for her husband's disappearance in the first place[342]. Among the Muslims, the decision of a half-widow to remarry often invites contentious theological debates, concerning the length of waiting period for a woman whose husband had disappeared.[343] In 1939, the dissolution of Mulsim Marriage Act was passed in India. It was adopted by the State of Jammu and Kashmir in the year 1942 and since then It prevails in J&K. There is a clause in the Act which

---

[340] ibid

[341] *Informative Missive* April 2006, p.11

[342] Half-life half widows; _http://kafilabackup.files.wordpress. com/2011/07/half-widow-half-wife-apdp.report.pdf_

[343] Muslims believe in 4 schools of thought, Hanafi, Malaki, shafifi and Hambli; according to hanfia school of thought, a woman has to wait for 90 years to remarry in case her husband disappeared. This lead Muslim Ulema of Hanafi School of Thought to think of an improvisation in the existing order therefore a clause was borrowed from Malaki school in which woman has to wait for 7 years, some say 4 and then she can remarry.

states; that a woman who is the wife of a person according to Muslim law shall be entitled to obtain a decree for the dissolution of marriage on the ground that the whereabouts of the husband have not been known for a period of 4 years. She can then go to court and seek permission to dissolve the marriage. Among the Muslim theologians, however, the issue is far from settled. One group of Ulema's in Kashmir say that if a half-widow, marries a second time and her first husband comes back, the previous marriage would be dissolved. However another group believe that if the first husband comes back after the woman has gone for a second marriage then the second marriage would be dissolved, but if she has borne any children from second marriage, they would be deemed legal[344].

Adding to the problems of these women, Personal laws do not allow distribution of property of a disappeared person unless he is 'declared' dead and surviving family members have to wait for 7 years to even apply in court to have some access to the property. The process takes another 2 years in court. Half widows and family, members of disappeared persons therefore have to wait at least 9 years before being able to access to property.[345] Remarriage is not an easy option for widows and half-widows, owing to the social stigma that is socially associated with it. Waiting for twelve years for her disappeared husband, Sara Bano married but faced social ostracism from her family and community[346]. A widow in her early thirties was encouraged by her acquaintances to

---

[344] *State of Human Rights in Jammu and Kashmir, 1990-2005*, p.277

[345] Afshana Rashid, *Half widows*. P. 96-97

[346] Sara Bano's testimony, in a study by Afsana, reveals that she married to feed her children as there was no other source of

remarry but she had to drop the idea on the ground that her in-laws, threatened to take custody of her two female-kids.[347] In a study conducted by Dabla, it has been shown that about 65% women retained the custody of their children, while the remaining 35% were forced to entrust their children to the care of their parental and maternal grand-parents.[348]. A report by APDP, points out that half-widows often suffer psychologically when they are separated from their children. There are several instances where the in-laws choose to keep and raise their grandchildren while turning out the half-widow and providing no visitation rights. In certain other cases, the half-widow's natal families take them back only on the condition that their children remain with the in-laws or be sent to orphanage. In still other cases, the report goes on to add, children are divided between the half-widow's parents and in-laws and she may in such a situation never see one/all of her children[349].

Many women who did remarry had to social ostracism, sometimes even from members of their own families.[350] Absence of organisations, both governmental and voluntary, working for such women, at the grass root level, has further worsened the plight.[351] Such hapless women sometimes

---

income and nobody helped her. But when she re-married. They kept taunting her.

[347] *Voices unheard* Vol -11, July- sep 2005

[348] Dabla Bashir Ahmad, *Widows and Orphans in Kashmir*, P.65

[349] Half-life Half -widow, *http://kafilabackup.files.wordpress.com/2011/07/half-widow-half-wife-apdp.report.pdf*

[350] Ibid

[351] Afsana Rashid, *Half-Widows,* p.12

resort to begging to feed their children[352]. Others take to prostitution selling their bodies to feed their families[353]. Adding to this, Dr Khurshid-ul-islam, 'since they do not have help from anywhere many women are compelled to enter flesh trade. In the absence of female politicians, women's concerns and aspirations remain hostage to a male-dominated Kashmiri polity and patriarchal militant leadership for whom gender is secondary'.[354] In 2004 sex scandal, a lady constable was alleged to be one among the pimps. On her arrest she revealed that the girls were also supplied to big hotels like Grand Palace and Hotel Broadway of Srinagar. She revealed that such girls were the ones who had recently been recruited in the dept. of Police and CID[355].

Rape affects the women's eligibility to marry or to remain married. In the infamous rape case in Kunan Pospora, only a couple of men took back their wives, even after intervention of the militants. Speaking to a women's group, a raped woman said that she begged her husband to forgive her for a sin she had never committed but he refused. He refused to take her back because he saw her as 'polluted' defiled by another man.[356] The marriage of raped women is

---

[352] Ten years ago Subi's husband, deputy chief of the Al-Barq militant outfit was killed by SF in an encounter. And this mother of six children lost everything. With no source of income, she was forced to beg in order to feed her children, among them a 20 year old unmarried daughter.

[353] Suri Kavita, *Impact of violence on women's education in Kashmir*, WISCOMP, New Delhi, 2006 p.39

[354] Kazi Seema, *Gender and Militarization*, p. 146

[355] Shabnum Qayoom, *Kashmir Mein Khwateen be-Hurmati*, Waqar Publications, Srinagar, edition 4, 2010, p. 299

[356] Urvashi Batalia(ed.) *Speaking peace, Women's Voices from Kashmir*, Kali for Women, New Delhi, 2002 p. 83

non-existent in Kashmir, but the stigma that is attached to rape, often prevent other girls in the family from finding a suitable groom.[357] The rape of women in Kunan Poshpora was a powerful symbolic defeat for the men of the village; yet, the sequential logic and politics of 'honour' transcended its perpetuators to rebound with cruel irony on its survivors. The men of Poshpora lament the fate that befell their women; yet when asked whether they would marry women from another village where women had been raped, they refuse categorically.[358]

Women are valued in Kashmir as markers of community identity, and the burden of preserving the cultural purity or Kashmir*iyat* falls on their bodies. Since women are seen as markers of community, identity, they are particularly vulnerable to violence and sexual abuse. Their vulnerability is heightened during times of conflict, and the battle among male contestants is mostly fought over women's bodies. Women's bodies are prime targets of attack, but women also suffer violence from their 'own men', as well, who impose restrictions on their movements and attire, in the interest of 'the honour of the community'[359]. Women in political struggles are configured as embodying the community/ nationality's distinct (superior) tradition and cultural identity. According to Rita Manchanda, the graphic representation of women's subordination as symbolised in the veil, exposes the gendered nature of the political struggles[360]. In Kashmir girl students complained that militants came to the class

---

[357]   *State of Human Rights in Jammu and Kashmir, 1990-05*, p.273
[358]   Kazi, Seema *Gender and Militarization*, 158
[359]   Ava& Rita *The Impact of Armed Conflict on Women*, p.18
[360]   Manchanda Rita, *Guns and Burqa* p.59

rooms and insisted that all girls cover their heads and wear *burqas*(veils).[361]

The Muslim fundamentalist organisations have been trying to introduce *burqa* and chador as part of their Islamisation programme. Notices were printed in the local papers warning women that severe action would be taken if they did not don *purdah*[362]. Such cultural violence against women actually serves to legitimise misogyny and a predatory construct of masculinity[363]. *The lashkare—toi-ba* decreed that Kashmiri women either 'wear *burqa*' (veil) or face bullets. Militants shot girls for wearing jeans and in doing so, argued that they actually 'protected women'.[364] Young students would also threaten a teacher who was not properly covered or had plucked her eye brows[365]. In march 1999, two Kashmiri girls, Mehvish(16 yr old) and Nausheen (14 yr old) were shot in

---

[361] *Rape and Molestation; A Weapon of War in Kashmir* (A consolidated report on atrocities committed on women in *Kashmir*) prepared by the Jammu and *Kashmir* Human Rights Awareness and Documentation Centre, Srinagar, No. 32(Srinagar: Institute of *Kashmir* Studies, 1998) 1998, p.39

[362] Urvashi Batalia(ed.) *Speaking Peace,* p.59

[363] Manchanda, Rita 'Guns and *Burqa*'p. 72

[364] Chenoy Anuradha, 'Resources or Symbols?' p. 184

[365] Women like Nayeema Ahmad Mehjoor, a radio star and executive producer with radio *Kashmir,* were under double pressure, to be veiled and to quit jobs denounced as un-Islamic. Nayema had colour thrown on her body by the *Purdah* crusaders. Amazingly people were swept up in a kind of blind faith that what Mujahids said was the voice of Allah. It is said that even her otherwise, non-conformist husband urged her to wear *burqa*. Cited from;, Manchanda Rita, *Guns and Burqa.*, p.59,

their legs by militants for wearing jeans[366]. The immediate resistance to a dress code came from the urban educated elite with college girls refusing to respond the militant threats. Their resistance received substantial support from Kashmiri women, especially in the rural areas, who found its imposition alien to their culture; *burqa* was never a part of traditional Kashmiri dress. Women would wear in the traditional attire of Kashmir a *qasaba* or ornate head gear and a long *phiran*, and their faces were never covered.[367]

Instead of protecting women *burqa* made these women more vulnerable to the security forces. Security forces were convinced that one in every three *burqa* clad person was a militant. It was believed that the disguise was used when militants wanted to shift hideouts. Women wearing *burqas* suffered humiliation and sexual harassment from the security forces.[368] In the process of enforcing dress code for women, the sari disappeared from the valley altogether.[369] The emphasis on *burqa* demonstrated an assertion by the men of the community of their control over their women, a protective control which had necessarily to be demonstrated given their sense of emasculation in the face of the armed might and humiliating treatment by security forces and their resentment towards women's necessary activism[370].

---

[366] Kavita Suri, *Impact of Violence on Education,* p.21

[367] Shiraz Sidhwa, "Dukhtaran-e-Millat: Profile of a militant, fundamentalist women's organisation," IN Kamla Bhasin and Ritu Menon (eds.), *Against All Odds: Essays on Women, Religion and Development from India and Pakistan*, New Delhi: Kali for Women, 1994, p.128

[368] Manchanda Rita,'Guns and *Burqa*' p.59,60

[369] Urvashi Batlalia(ed.), *Speaking Peace* P.138

[370] Chenoy Anuradha, 'Resources or Symbols?'., p.184

Under the continued threat of the militants and conservative elements in Kashmir, almost all women have taken to *burqa* or chador. There is scarcely any woman in the valley who would walk around in public places without covering her head[371]. By and large girls in Kashmir no longer wear skirts or jeans[372]. I enquired from my respondents about their opinions over the impact of diktats on the dress of Kashmiri women. 44.5% women respondents said that *purdah* has become mandatory for women in Kashmir and 18% of the total respondents said that covering of heads has become compulsory after the issue of diktat. However Respondents believed that there was no impact of diktats on the attire of women in Kashmir.

---

[371] Manchanda 'Guns and *Burqa*'. p.59
[372] Ibid p.87

APPENDIX III-A

STATE AS AGGRESSOR

A Report in the Newsletter of an NGO (2005)

Zahida was killed by a Rashtriya Rifles soldier masked as a militant, whom he intended to rape, in the intervening night of 13 and 14 July 2005 at around 11PM. The soldier had entered the house through window after the inmates refused to allow him into the house. When the inmates screamed he fired at and stabbed Zahida, and fled from the house while spraying bullets at the chasing villagers. CRPF troopers manning in the paddy fields thought he was a militant and gunned him down. Later dead soldier was identified as Baljinder Singh of 49 Rashtriya Rifles.

While talking to *Voices Unheard,* the family members said that at 11.05 PM on Wednesday night. They heard someone knocking at their door. 'We heard a knock at the door but did not respond to it. For we knew that, at this point of time no civilian would dare to move out of his home'. However, he climbed a walnut tree adjacent to our house and jumped into our compound. His face was veiled. He was in civvies,' said Muhammed Iqbal, younger brother of Zahida. Iqbal was the first person to identify the veiled intruder as the RR personnel. The soldier was stationed adjacent to the victim's house on 12th July when RR person cordoned the whole village.

APPENDIX III-B

SRO 43

Application of Rules:-These rules shall apply to the Compassionate appointment of a person who is a family member of:-

i. a Government employee who dies in harness other than due to militancy related action;
ii. a Government employee who dies as a result of militancy related action and is not involved in militancy related activities;
iii. a civilian who dies as a result of militancy related action not involved in militancy related activities and total income of the family from all sources does not exceed Rs.3,500/—per month as assessed by the Revenue Officer not below the rank of an Assistant Commissioner;
iv. A permanent resident Junior Commissioned Officer or non-Commissioned Officer of the armed force or an Officer of equivalent rank of the Para military force who is killed in action connected with law and order duties within the State of Jammu and Kashmir or as a result of enemy action on the line of actual control.

Source: Office of the Divisional Commissioner, Government of J&K *http://kashmirdivision.nic.in/about/services/sro43a.htm*

APPENDIX III-C

JAMMU AND KASHMIR PUBLIC SAFETY ACT, 1978 (ACT NO. 6 OF 1978)

Excerpts

1) Government may, by notified order, declare any place to be a prohibited place.

2) No person shall, without the permission of the Government or the authority specified by the Government, enter, or be on or in, or pass any prohibited place.

3) Any person is granted permission to enter, or to be on or in, or to pass over, a prohibited place, that person shall, while acting under such permission comply with such orders for regulating his conduct as may be given by the authority specified by the Government.

4) Any Police Officer, or any other person authorised in this behalf by the Government, may search any person entering or seeking to enter or being on or in, or leaving a prohibited place, and any vehicle, ... , and may, for the purpose of the search, detain such person, vehicle, aircraft and article.

Provided that no female shall be searched in pursuance of this sub—section except by a female . . . .

Source: Laws of India

http://www.lawsofindia.org/statelaw/6389/ TheJammuandKashmirPublicSafetyAct1978.html

CHAPTER IV

WOMEN'S ROLE IN THE POLITICS OF RESISTANCE IN KASHMIR

Women's Agency

S ociological theories usually deal with stable societies, and while sociologists study violence as a social problem, they rarely engage with societies where people suffer violence in almost every day, routine forms. Most sociological concepts turn out to be inadequate in dealing with conflict-ridden societies, where violence is an almost daily occurrence. Sociologists who have studied conflict-ridden societies usually treat women as passive, inert victims of violence. While it is indeed true that in situations of violent conflict women are systematically targeted, and suffer far more than men, they also exercise considerable agency in such situations.

In situations of conflict and armed struggles, it is often their reproductive and nurturing roles that are politicised. Rita Manchanda rightly points out that the political activities of ordinary women arise from their everyday experiences, of affirming concern for the safety of their family and the sustenance of their community. The populist demands of the struggle created the social space for women to come out of their domestic seclusion[373]. Several Studies have shown that in situations of conflict women take on new independent roles and demonstrate capacities for decision making with implications for at least, equal involvement of women in community management, peace process and reconstruction activities[374].

While challenging the notion of victimhood in the midst of war, the women of Kashmir are engaged in reconstructing their devastated lives. As Rita Manchanda holds, in war, the dominant image of women as losers—as victims, has grave consequences for a true awareness of the differential impact of conflict on women's and men's lives and the creative strategies that women forge for the survival of their families and communities. The hardships and struggles for survival pushes them into assuming decision—making roles, sometimes as participants in peace negotiations and other times, as active agents in the armed conflict. The challenge is to shore up the 'gains' wrought by conflict in the experiences

---

[373] Manchanda Rita(ed.), *Women, War and Peace in South Asia; Beyond Victimhood to Agency,* Sage Publications, New Delhi,2001 pp.57

[374] Manchanda Rita, 'Women's Agency in Peace building; Gender Relations in Post-Conflict Construction, *Economic and Political Weekly,*—Vol.40, No.44/45, (Oct 29-Nov 4) 2005, p.1437

of both civilian and combatant women to strengthen women as agents of social transformation. It is a paradox that even as armed conflict cause immense pain and sufferings to women, these conflict creates spaces for women to assert their agency, and actively reshape their personal and social relationships, and political commitments.[375]

Women of Kashmir came out from their homes, in the early days of 1990 protesting against the atrocities of the state, and to shield men from the *lathis* of the forces. They would sit on daily *dharnas* in large groups at the city's jails to pressurise the security forces to free the boys who had been picked up, often arbitrarily by the forces. Women seized the democratic space for popular protest and would march to the UN office, out in front, shielding the men, braving *lathi* blows and tear gas. It was an activism rooted in their cultural role as mothers, wives and sisters[376]. Rita Manchanda argues that domestic activism rests on the 'Stretched roles' of women's everyday lives as caregivers and nurtures and is often ignored in the narratives of political struggles. Women develop the habit of listening to the news and staying connected to the informal grapevine[377]. Consciousness leads to activism, and

---

[375] Manchanda Rita, 'Women's Agency in Peace building; Gender Relations in Post-Conflict Construction, *Economic and Political Weekly*,—Vol.40, No.44/45, (Oct 29-Nov 4) 2005, p.4738

[376] Manchanda, Rita 'Guns and *Burqa*: Women in the *Kashmir*i Conflict', in Manchanda (ed.) *Women, War and Peace in South Asia; Beyond Victimhood to Agency*), Sage Publications, New Delhi, 2001

[377] Manchanda, Women's Agency in Peace building; Gender Relations in Post-Conflict Construction, *Economic and Political Weekly*,—Vol.40, No.44/45, (Oct 29-Nov 4) 2005 p.4739

as they become politically conscious, they are constrained to involve themselves in public and political spaces as well. The popular demand for *Azadi* or the Kashmir *intifada*, created an ambiguous space for women's assertion. While old and young men, fearing crackdowns, shoot-outs and torture withdrew from the public eye, women captured the public centre-stage to ensure the survival of their families. They learnt to negotiate power for the safety of their families and to secure in the release of their men. In an unusual 'stretching' of domestic roles, women assumed political roles, and actively participated with forces of political resistance. Even though women gain agency, armed conflict emasculates society and reinforces sexist roles[378]. As observed by scholars studying in Palestine, armed conflict leads to the blurring of the boundaries that separate the home from the front, and collapses distinctions between feminine and masculine spaces in conflict. The continuous violation of the home-the violent entries, searches and demolitions, sieges and massacre of civilians cast aside notions of home as a space distant from the conflict[379]. As observed by Seema Kazi, the Kashmiri women's engagement with the Movement for *Azadi* derives from their own understanding and lived experience of the situation that testifies to not just a keen political understanding of the crisis, but their multiple roles within it. She further argues that these multiple roles of women have

---

[378] Bhawana Khajooria, 'Political Roles of Women in Kashmir' IN, Malashri Lal, Sukrita Paul Kumar (ed.) *Women's studies in India, contours of change,* Indian Institute of advanced study, Shimla 2002, p. 270

[379] Julie Peteet, 'Icons and Militants: Mothering in the Danger Zone', IN, Therese, Carolyn, Allen, (ed.) Op.cit138

preserved family and community, and greatly facilitated the general resistance against state hegemony[380].

Domestic activism of women is vital, for, the sustenance of the conflict. It is women who keep intact the fabric of the family and community which enables the men to go on fighting. There were hundreds ordinary women who organised food supply lines during the months of unbroken curfew. in 1991, there was an uninterrupted curfew for 190 days[381] and in the 2008 2009 and the 2010 uprisings[382] in Kashmir, it was women who were actually managing the families and even struggling against the arrests of youth in Kashmir during what was termed as 'new Kashmir *intifada*'. At the same time they participated in stone pelting, and gave moral support to the boys to carry on the fight with stones. Women thus again took to the streets in large numbers, walking alongside the men, raising pro-Kashmiri independence slogans, in defiance of the security forces that surrounded them[383].

In the face of continued violence, women have made efforts to break the silence, calling for accountability,

---

[380] Kazi Seema, *Between Democracy and Nation-Gender and Militarization in Kashmir,* Women Unlimited, New Delhi,2005, p. 142

[381] Manchanda Rita,'Guns and Burqa' . p.52

[382] In 2008, 2009, 2010, Violent Conflict, Kashmir was shut for months together

[383] Arundhati Roy, "Land and Freedom," *The Guardian,* 22 August 2008; Lydia Polgreen, "2 Killings Stroke Kashmiri Rage at Indian Force*," The New York Times*, 15 August 2009; Parvaiz Bukhari, "Kashmir 2010: The Year of Killing Youth," *The Nation*,22 September 2010.

disarmament and restoration of peace. While women were not active combatants, many supported the Movement in the 1990's.[384] Their support for the armed struggle has drastically diminished in the recent decades and given way to peaceful protests and consciousness-raising activities. Women in Kashmir organised demonstrations and marches to protest the arrest or disappearance of their sons and husbands. Akin to what has been observed in Palestine, they were, through demonstrations actually protesting against the disruption and chaos of everyday domestic life occasioned by the disappearance of loved ones as well as concern for their well-being.[385] The unflinching courage of marginalised women like Parveena Ahangar, in their fight for justice symbolises the self-actualisation of Kashmiri women, in the face of continued violence and suffering. Her activism lead to the formation of an organisation, in 1994, named Association of Parents of Disappeared persons (APDP). Parveena Ahangar became the founding member of APDP and was chosen as its president. It comprised of the parents of individuals subjected to enforced disappearances. APDP now has members from 150 families. Women constitute 60% of membership, have 50% representation on the executive board (5 out of 10 rotating members are women) and at least 50% representation during monthly public protests[386].

---

[384] See e.g: Urvashi Batalia, *Speaking Peace, Women's Voices from Kashmir,* Kali for Women, New Delhi, 2002

[385] Julie Peteet 'Icons and Militants; Mothering in a Danger Zone', p. 139

[386] Half Widow-Half life, Responding to Gendered Violence in Kashmir, A report by Association of Parents of Disappeared persons, *http://kafilabackup.files.wordpress.com/2011/07/half-widow-half-wife-apdp.report.pdf* accessed on 20th August, 2011

Recently, APDP found the graves of 1,000 unidentified corpses, unceremoniously dug, in graveyards across Uri, the de-facto frontier region that divides Indian and Pakistani controlled Kashmir. Despite its meagre sources APDP has made strong case for an independent international scientific investigation.[387] According to APDP's own records 8000 to 10,000 people have been subjected to enforced disappearances during different regimes.[388]

As service provider women also run orphanages, self help groups in the conflict torn Kashmir. Nighat Pandit (born 1961) stepped out of a comfortable home to address the pain and trauma of people caught in the conflict. Braving physical danger and other risks, Pandit and her organisation HELP (human efforts for love and peace)[389] and inter-communal harmony. At a time when very few Kashmiri women were responding to the crisis in their midst, Pandit was the first woman to start an orphanage (in 1997) for homeless children. Pandit makes personal visits to violence-affected areas and interviews the people. She also works with groups

---

[387] *http://www.greaterKashmir.com/news/2008/Mar/31/grave-concern-23.asp* Accessed on March 10,2010

[388] Afsana Rashid, *Waiting for Justice- Half-widows* P.18-19

[389] HELP foundation works to provide relief to those worst affected by the conflict. The main activities of the organisations are the education and upbringing of orphans, the rehabilitation of widows, mental health counselling for women and children, and the rehabilitation of physically-and visually challenged children. She runs '*Shahjar*', an orphanage and her own school and counselling centre. Her children had to leave the valley at a young age because they were threatened with kidnapping.

to organise income-generating projects.[390] Miss Anjum Zamruda Habib, who heads a Women's organisation in Kashmir, after spending five years of vigorous Jail term, on release founded the Association of Kashmiri Prisoners (AFKP). AFKP provides psycho-social support to the families of Kashmiri prisoners held in Indian jails, as well as tracking and documenting their cases[391].

No peace Movement in the world has succeeded without women's activism. Women in several conflict areas have played a pivotal role in giving a much needed push to the peace process. Even in south Asian conflict, such as Srilanka, women are creating their own niche trying to propel the peace process forward.[392].

One of the interesting developments in Kashmir has been the appropriation of literary space by women to push forward the agenda of peace. Women in Kashmir have unsuccessfully tried their hand in literary activism. One such attempt was made by a group of women activists 'Kashmiri Women's Initiative for Peace and disarmament (KWIPD)' who used to chronicle women's narratives in a quarterly newsletter 'Voices

---

[390] Bhadhuri Aditi, Creating New Lives In Kashmir's Conflict Zone, *Social welfare* August 2009, 56(5) p.24-25, also see, Fearless Nighat, *Social Welfare,* September 2007 p.12

[391] The militant in her: Women and Resistance
http://www.aljazeera.com/indepth/spotlight/ kashmirtheforgottenconflict/2011/07/2011731995821770.html

[392] Half Widow-Half life, Responding to Gendered Violence in Kashmir, A Report by Association of Parents of Disappeared persons, *http://kafilabackup.files.wordpress.com/2011/07/half-widow-half-wife-apdp.report.pdf*

Unheard'[393]. It was focused mainly on the victimhood. In another effort Saima Farhad and Sheeba Masoodi Launched a women's Magazine named 'SHE'. In the inaugural issue of SHE, the editors explained that the magazine would be an effort to unravel the talent and courage of women in Kashmir. They also claimed that this would provide the women a platform to discuss about their rights[394]. Both the attempts have failed, apparently, due to insufficient resources available to them.

Women in secessionist/political and militant Movements:

Studies on Kashmir show that Women's Movements in Kashmir is deeply entangled with, either aligned with or engaged with the secessionist Movements. As has been argued by Alison, the ethno-nationalist political Movements everywhere impinge on gender roles, and crucially shape the experiences and aspirations of women. It has been suggested in several important works on separatist and/or secessionist Movements, anti-state Movements generally provide greater ideological and political spaces for women to articulate their political agency, and even participate as combatants than

---

[393] JKCCS Pays Tribute to Asia on her First Death Anniversary, *Voices Unheard,* Vol:10, April-June 2005, P.2 also see, *http://www.Kashmirglobal.com/2011/09/Half-Widow-Half-Wife-APDP.full-report.pdf,*

[394] She is first to hit the news stand, *Greater* Kashmir, 09, April, 2006, Also see; Silent awakening among Kashmiri women *www.expressindia.com/news/fullstory.php?newsid=71828*

do institutionalised state or prostate nationalism[395]. Several studies, and press reports reveal that in the initial years of militancy in Kashmir, women joined militants and acted as couriers for them. Little suspected by the armed forces, they were initially, at least, a crucial asset to the militants. But once the armed forces came to know that these women were facilitating safe passage for militants and their ammunition, the coercive arm of the state did not spare them, and security forces have routinely targeted them, raping, molesting, and eliminating them. The 'rage of the state', as it were, has not spared innocent women either, and the violence perpetrated by the armed forces has showed a remarkable indifference in distinguishing the aggressors and the victim[396]. The pressure from militants, assisted by the violence of the state, has led to the emergence of several political Movements among women, and a few among them, indeed, do seem to enjoy a wide social base.[397] Several feminist scholars have argued that feminism has had a difficult relationship with wars[398]. In conflict-ridden regions in India, such as Nagaland and Manipur, women cadres are present in significant numbers in most of the insurgent and national liberation groups[399]. In Kashmir, on the other hand, some women's organisations

---

[395] Alison Merinda 'Women as Agents of Political Violence: Gendering Security', *Security Dialogue*, 35, 447-463, 2004

[396] Maqbool Sahil, 'Tehreke-Mazahamat Mein Khuwatein ka Role -1', IN, *Tanazaaye Kashmir* Vol-1 p.384

[397] Ibid p. 385

[398] Cooke, Mariam and Angela Woolacott (ed. 1993) *Gendering War Talk* Princeton New Jersey; Princeton University Press) p. 181

[399] Chenoy Anuradha.M., 'Resources or symbols? Women and Armed conflict in India' IN Ava Darshan Shrestha and Rita Thapa(ed.), *The Impact of Armed Conflict on Women In South Asia*, Manohar, 2007, p. 194

defending extremist positions exist, but women are not represented in the existing political organisations of the militants. These organisations are fed by intolerant religious ideologies, and routinely propagate jihad against India[400].

Muslim *Khawateen-e-Markaz*

Muslim Khwateen-e-Markaz (MKM), one of the prominent Women's Organisation in Kashmir, is being headed by Zamruda Habib and Yasmeen Raja. In late 1980's, as an organisation it was, during this period of its inception, linked to the Islamic Students League, a puritan Movement based the ideology of religious revivalism.[401]

Zamruda Habib was a lecturer at Hanfia College Anantnag (also known as Islamabad) when she formed a group of like—minded educated women, named 'Women's Association', perhaps the first of its kind after independence from Dogra Rule. Led by educated women, the association represented the interests and aspirations of middle class women in Kashmir[402].

The constitution of MKM (See Appendices IVA and IVB) was framed by Ms. Zamruda Habib and her associate Zaheer-u-Din.

---

[400] Ibid, P.196
[401] Maqbool Sahil 'Tehreke-Mazahamat me Khwateen ka role-1' p. 389
[402] ibid

The Constitution of the MKM, in its Part second (clause 5), sets following aims and objectives of the party.

I) It shall be the duty of MKM to strive for a solution of the Kashmir Issue. The political aspirations of Kashmiri's should be fulfilled in accordance with the Charter of International Human Rights.

II) It shall struggle for the political, economic, social, legal, educational, cultural and religious rights of the Women in Jammu and Kashmir.

   a) It shall patronise and encourage in the field of art and education.

   b) It shall focus on the problems of women from backward classes in the valley and work for their upliftment.

MKM proposes a democratic republic structure for the party, limiting its membership to 51. The constitution also directs the party to set-up municipal and village committees, Block committees and halqa committees in order to reach out at the grass roots level.

Dukhtarane-Millat

When the conflict broke in Kashmir in 1990, Asiya Andrabi came in the forefront with her women's organisation called *Dukhtarane-millat* (DeM)[403]. The main objectives of DeM, as claimed[404] by Asiya Andrabi's, are:

1. To make Muslim women aware of their rights in Islam
2. To support the separatist Movements in-order to carve an Islamic state or accede to Pakistan so that an Islamic Sharia be enacted on all Muslim Men and Women of the state.

The DeM strongly advocates and campaigns for the establishment of Islamic State in Kashmir[405]. Asiya says, 'I don't believe in *Kashmiriyat* for me there are only two

---

[403] Born in 1962 and brought up in Srinagar, she did her graduation in Home science from Kashmir University in 1981. She dreamt of becoming a scientist and wanted to go for higher education outside the state. Her elder brother denied her the permission to go for higher studies outside Kashmir and she was forced to remain in the four walls of her home. Incidentally Asiya's eyes once fell on a book '*Khwateen ke dilon ki batein*'. The book was about the rights of Muslim women and after reading this book, Asiya's life changed forever. She later decided to live her life according to the Shariat laws and struggle for the rights of Muslim women in Kashmir. As a result, she founded 'DeM'. Cited from Sahil Maqbool, *Tehreke-Mazahamat me Khwateen Ka role.*

[404] It has not been possible for the researcher to get a copy of their constitution as it has been banned since 2002

[405] Prahar Swati, Gender Jihad Jingoism; Women as perpetrators, planners and patrons of militancy in Kashmir, *Studies in Conflict Terrorism,* Volume:34, issue:4, TAYLOR & FRANCIS, 2011, p.303

communities one Muslim and other non-Muslim'.[406]
Thus the essence of *Kashmiriyat* has no place in Andrabi's
Pan-Islamist World view. She clearly rejects the notions of
Indian or even Pakistani nationality.

There are other organisations, which did not survive and
little is known about them. The Hizbul-Mujahidin (HM),
one of the major militant outfits, also established a women's
wing, the *Binat-ul-Islam*, led by Umi-Arifa. Members of
this group would visit families of slain militants and assist
them rehabilitation and relief.[407]. Another lesser known
militant women's organisation was, *Banaat-e-Aaiyesha*. This
organisation was an offshoot of Jaishe-e.Mohammed, and
claimed to represent women's interests within the militant
organisation[408].

MKM and DeM have a political mandate professing
separation from India while, in addition, carrying out social
and Human Rights activism.

It has been argued by several feminist scholars, in particular,
Swati Prahar, that the organisations such as DeM have served
to provide political agency to women in Kashmir[409]. While
this is certainly true to an extent, we should not ignore the

---

[406] Maqbool Sahil, 'Tehreke-Mazahamt me Khwateen ka role-1',
p. 386

[407] Muzammil Jaleel Spawning Militancy: The Rise Of Hizbul 22
May 2003 *The Indian Express* http://www.jammu-Kashmir.com/
archives/archives2003/Kashmir20030522d.html

[408] ibid

[409] Jihad Jingoism; Women as perpetrators, planners and
patrons of militancy in Kashmir, *Studies in Conflict Terrorism*,
Volume:34, issue:4, TAYLOR & FRANCIS, 2011 p. 304

fact that women's agency is often involved to serve ends that are anti-women and deeply patriarchal. To take the case of DeM, it is a women's organisation avowedly concerned with women's issues in Kashmir. At the same-time, it is not averse to rely on coercion and force to impose its world view-fundamentalist and Puritan-on the women in Kashmir. Furthermore, its agenda for reforms of women is deeply entangled with patriarchal values, and emphasizes segregation for women. It is to take recourse to force to pressurise women to adopt veil and *purdah* in their lives. Like other right wing, fundamentalist organisations, members of DeM are actively involved in moral policing activities. In their role as moral policewomen, women in DeM have often targeted locations they see as 'centres of immoral activities'. The list of places deemed 'immoral' is, of course, quite large, and ever expanding; it includes cafes, restaurants, liquor shops, hotels, internet cafes and even gift shops[410].

The ideology of DeM actually serves to reinforce gender inequities, and gender division of labour. The leaders of DeM admit to the subordinate position of women, and see the role of women to lie in the organisation of families, procreation and child-bearing activities[411]. At the same time, DeM is actively involved in political activities, and vigorously campaign for the creation of new political order in Kashmir based on their version of Islam[412]. One clearly notices a paradox here, one that several scholars have noticed in other

---

[410] Ibid 303

[411] M.Mazharul Haque, 'Profile: Aisya Andrabi: Warrior in Veil,' *The Milii Gazette* 3(17) (1-15 September 2002). *www. miligazette.com/archives/01092002/0109200264.htm*

[412] See Maqbool Sahil, *Tehreke-Mazahamahat me Khwateen ka role vol-1*

women's militant social outfits-the push towards political activism goes hand-in-hand with the normative privileging of the place of women in the family/household. Indeed, as has been suggested by Swati Prahar[413], militant Movements everywhere succeed in mobilising, even incorporating, certain varieties of women's Movement, particularly those that are based on forms of religious identifications.

Conclusion

This chapter has revealed that women have shown tremendous resilience in combating the culture of violence, organising themselves in movements and organisations through which they participate in the political process and create spaces for constructive political communication. There is, however, some cause of concern in the way the wome's organisations in Kashmir have been participating in the poltical process. My concern emerges from the drift towards religious extremism that seems to have swayed many of these organisations. This is probably a strategy to become a part of dominant political dialogue but it has lead to their further political dialogue but it has lead to their further political marginalisation. Women's organisations should be primarily engaged in promoting the women's rights. In Kashmir Women's organisations should be primarily engaged in promoting the women's rights. In Kashmir women organisations have mostly failed to adhere to their main objectives and have scarcely addressed themselves to social problems of women in general.

---

[413] Prahar Swati, Gender Jihad and Jingoism,

Scholars like Tanika Sarkar have shown that in the wake of globalization of Indian economy and society there has not only been a resurgence of militarism but also an increase in the participation of women in these militant activities. This chapter has shown the relevance of thesis in the case of Kashmir, where there has been, since the 1980's, increased involvement of women in militant political activities. I have argued that militant women, indeed, reproduce patriarchal ideologies, but their participation has also served to enhance spaces of dialogue and communication in the political spaces. Furthermore, in the culture of militancy and violence, women, in the both formal and informal ways, have applied the healing touch, providing crucial services to individuals and families destroyed by violence, this chapter also highlighted the role of women in peace-building operations. Even as there are instances of women participating/ supporting militancy, however, there is also evidence of women confronting militancy, as well. In either case, indeed, the women in Kashmir have been vehemently asserting their presence in the political domains.

APPENDIX IV-A

CONSTITUTION OF JAMMU AND KASHMIR
MUSLIM KHWATEEN MARKAZ

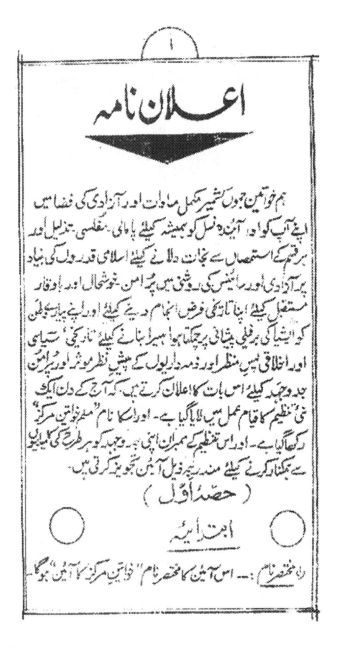

۲

(۲) تنظیم کا نام :۔ اس آئین کے تحت تشکیل شدہ تنظیم کا نام
"مسلم خواتین مرکز" ہوگا۔

(۳) شناختی نشان :۔ اس کا شناختی نشان آسمانی رنگ
کا پرچم ہوگا۔ اور اس میں سبز رنگ کے علاوہ سفید ہلال ہوگا۔

(۴) صدر دفتر اور دائرہ اثر :۔ تنظیم کا صدر دفتر سری نگر میں
ہوگا۔ اور اسکی تنظیمی کارکردگیوں
کا دائرہ اس آئین کے مقررہ کردہ حدود کے اندر ہوگا۔

(حصّہ دوم)

اغراض و مقاصد

(۵) تنظیم کے اغراض و مقاصد :۔ اس تنظیم کی سپہرم کروشل
گزشتہ اٹھائیس سال کے حالات و واقعات کا مسلسل اور مکمل
جائزہ لینے کے بعد اس امر کو شدت کے ساتھ محسوس کرتی ہے کہ ہمارے
کشمیر کو کہ ہماری ریاست کی تعمیر و ترقی اور امن و استحکام کی راہ میں
ایک زبردست رکاوٹ بن چکا ہے کا فوری لعود پر عمل ہونا چاہیے
تاکہ ریاست کا مستقبل یقینی بن جائے اور عوام المسلمان کا سانس
لے سکیں۔ اس سلسلے میں "مسلم خواتین مرکز" برصغیر میں امن و
استحکام اور دوستی کی فضا کو قائم کرنے کے لیے ہندوستان۔
پاکستان اور کشمیر کے نمائندوں پر مشتمل ایک مہم غربیقی کانفرنس کے
انعقاد کو ترجیح دیتی ہے۔ جس میں بین الاقوامی چارٹرکے تحت

167

مسئلہ حقوق انسانی کے اعلان نامہ کی بنیاد پر یہ طے کیا جائے
کہ مسئلہ کشمیر کو حل کرنے کیلئے ریاستی عوام کو حق خود ارادیت
کا استعمال کرنے کیلئے کونسا طریقہ وضع کیا جائے۔

(۶) ریاست جموں و کشمیر کی خواتین کے سیاسی، اقتصادی،
سماجی، قانونی، قلمی، تہذیبی اور مذہبی حقوق کے تحفظ
کیلئے جدوجہد۔

(الف) جس میں ہر قسم کی فنکار اور صاحب علم عورتوں کی ہمت
افزائی ہو۔ (ب) ریاست کے پیمانہ؟ قبیلوں اور علاقوں
میں عورتوں کی مشکلات اور تکالیف کا اندازہ کرنے کے ذرائع
پر خصوصی توجہ۔ اور انکو اپنے پاؤں پر کھڑا ہونے کے طریقے
وضع کرنا۔

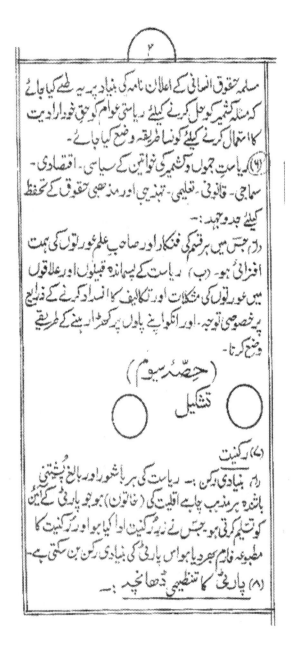

(حصّہ سوم)

تشکیل

(۷) رکنیت
راہ بنیادی رکن ؟۔۔ ریاست کی ہر باشعور اور بالغ پشتینی
باشندہ ہر مذہب چاہے اقلیت کی (خاتون) ہو جو پارٹی کے یقین
کو تسلیم کرتی ہو۔ جس نے نذر رکنیت ادا کیا ہو اور رکنیت کا
مطبوعہ فارم بھر دیا ہو اس پارٹی کی بنیادی رکن بن سکتی ہے۔

(۸) پارٹی کا تنظیمی ڈھانچہ ؟۔۔

(ر) محلہ یا دیہہ کمیٹی :۔ سرینگر کے ہر محلہ میں محلہ کمیٹی ودیہات
کے ہر گاؤں میں ایک دیہہ کمیٹی ہوگی جو زیادہ سے نیا پچیس گیارہ
ممبروں پر مشتمل ہوگی اور اسکی صدر، نائب صدر، سیکریٹری
اور خزانچی انہی علاقوں کی خواتین باشندہ ممبروں نے منتخب
کی ہوگی۔

ہر محلہ/دیہہ کمیٹی جزلا کونسل کیلئے اپنے ڈیلیگیٹ بھیجا کرے گی
محلہ/دیہہ کمیٹی کی صدر نامزدہ ڈیلیگیٹ ہوگی اور باقی ڈیلیگیٹ
اسی گاؤں کی ممبر منتخب کرے گی۔ یہی ڈیلیگیٹ اعلیٰ سطح کی
تنظیمی کمیٹیوں کا انتخابی ادارہ تشکیل دیں گی۔

(ب) علاقائی کمیٹی یا حلقہ کمیٹی :۔
(۱) ایک بلاک میں کئی گاؤں پر مشتمل حلقہ کمیٹیاں ہوں گی جنکی
تعداد اور حد بندی سے متعلق زونل کمیٹی کی تنظیمی باڈی وقتاً فوقتاً
کرتی ہوگی۔

(۲) حلقہ کمیٹی کی خواتین ایکان متعلقہ دیہات اور محلہ کمیٹیوں
کی خواتین ڈلی کیٹیوں پر مشتمل ہوگی۔

(۳) حلقہ کمیٹی کی تنظیمی باڈی گیارہ ممبران پر مشتمل ہوگی جنا
میں ڈلی کیٹوں کی منتخب کی ہوئی صدر۔ نائب صدر سیکریٹری
اور خزانچی شامل ہوگی۔

(ج) بلاک کمیٹی :۔
فا ہر تنظیمی بلاک میں ایک کمیٹی ہوگی جس میں بشمول صدر

۵

نائب صدور، سکریٹری، جوائنٹ سکریٹری اور خزانچی کل
اکیس ممبر ہوں گی جن کو بلاک کے اس انتخابی ادارے نے منتخب
کیا ہو۔ یعنی یہ کمیٹی کی ڈولی گیٹوں، حلقہ کمیٹیوں کی صدور، نا
اور سکریٹریوں پر مشتمل ہو گا۔

(ہ) ذیلی کمیٹی :۔۔

(د) تنظیمی زون دربا ستی مجلس عاملہ کے مقرر کردہ بلاکوں
کی مناسب تعداد پر مشتمل ہو گا۔

(اا) ہر تنظیمی زون کے لیے اکیس ممبروں پر مشتمل ایک کمیٹی
ہو گی جیسے صدر، نائب صدر، سکریٹری، جوائنٹ سکریٹری،
پبلسٹی سکریٹری اور خزانچی کو بلاک کا اجتماعی ادارہ چنیں گے۔
یہ ودہیم/محلہ کمیٹیوں کے ڈیلیگیٹوں، بلاک اور حلقہ کمیٹیوں کے
صدور اور سکریٹریوں پر مشتمل ہو گا۔

(س) ریاستی مجلس عاملہ :۔۔

(ا) ریاستی مجلس عاملہ ہو کی ریاست کی سطح پہ ایک تنظیمی
باڈی نما ہو گی۔ تمام ذیلی کمیٹیاں بلا راست اسی تنظیم کے ماتحت
ہوں گی۔

(اا) یہ تنظیم زیادہ سے زیادہ اکیس ممبروں پر مشتمل ہو گی۔
جس کا انتخاب اور نامزدگی بطریق ذیل ہو گی۔

(ا) ہر زونل خاتون صدر اس تنظیم کی نامزد ممبر ہو گی۔

(ب) ہر زون کی ڈیلیگیٹ خواتین صدر کے علاوہ ایک اور ممبر

۶

کوہ پیاستی تنظیم کیے منتخب کریں گی۔

(ج) باقی ممبران صدر کے ذریعہ نامزد ہوں گی بشرطیکہ یہ تعداد کسی بھی صورت میں دس سے زیادہ نہ ہو۔

نیز پیاستی تنظیم کے عام انتخابات پارٹی کے آئین کے تحت مکمل ہونے تک پہ تنظیم زیادہ سے زیادہ اکتیس ممبروں پہ مشتمل ہوگی جن میں سے پندرہ ممبر میڈم چیپر پرسن (صدر مختصر) کی نامزد کی ہوئی ہوں۔

(الف) پیاستی مجلس عاملہ میں مندرجہ ذیل عہدہ دار ہوں گی۔

(ر) میڈم چیپر پرسن	۱	
(ب) نائب چیپر پرسن	۳	
(ج) جنرل سکریٹری	۳	
(د) اسسٹنٹ سکریٹری	۱	
(ہ) سکریٹری	۱	
(س) خزانچی	۱	
(ش) آرگنائزر	۱	

(س) جنرل کونسل :۔

(الف) دیہہ/محلہ کمیٹیوں کی تمام ڈیلیگیٹ اور دیگر ماتحت کمیٹیوں کی صدور اور سکریٹریوں پر مشتمل ایک جنرل کونسل ہوگی جو سب سے اعلیٰ تنظیمی ادارہ ہوگا اور آئینی دفعات کے تحت پارٹی پہ خفیہ گنتری وؤں کا مجاز ہوگا۔

٧

(١١) جنرل کونسل ریاستی مجلس عاملہ کا انتخابی ادارہ ہوگا۔

(۹) تنظیمی کمیٹیوں کی کارکردگی اور اختیارات :۔

اس آئین کے تحت پارٹی کی مختلف کمیٹیوں کی کارکردگی اور
اختیارات حسب ذیل ہونگے۔

(ا) ریاستی مجلس عاملہ کی کارکردگی اور اختیارات :۔
(ا) پارٹی کے اغراض و مقاصد کو موثر بنانے کیلئے قواعدو
ضوابط کا وضع کرنا۔

(١١) تمام ماتحت زونل، بلاک و دیگر کمیٹیوں کا کنٹرول۔
(١١١) اس آئین کے عملی اقدامات کیلئے طریقہ کار اور اصول
وضع کرنا اور جو اصول پارٹی کے آئین کے خلاف ہو اسکو
کالعدم قرار دینا۔

(١٧) مخصوص معاملات کیلئے سب کمیٹیوں کی تشکیل۔

(٧) پارٹی کے ذرائع آمدنی اور مصارف کے قواعد و
ضوابط مقرر کرنا۔

(٧١) پارٹی کے آئینی حدود کے اندر تمام کارکردگیوں اور
اختیارات کی عمل آوری۔

ریاستی مجلس عاملہ اپنے کچھ اختیارات کسی زون یا
بلاک کو بھی اسی زون یا بلاک کی حدود کے اندر نافذ کرنے کیلئے
منتقل کرنے کی مجاز ہوگی۔

۸

(vii) مرکزی انتخابی بورڈ کی تشکیل و تنظیم ۔

(ب) جنرل کونسل کی کارکردگی اور اختیارات :۔

(i) ریاستی مجلس عاملہ کے سمیت تمام تنظیمی اکائیوں کا کنٹرول

(ii) ریاستی مجلس عاملہ کے پیش کردہ منصوبوں اور پالیسیوں پر بحث و تمحیص اور ان کی منظوری ۔

(iii) ریاستی مجلس عاملہ کے وضع کردہ ضوابط آمد و خرچ پر غور و خوض کرنا ۔

(iv) ریاستی مجلس عاملہ کے وضع کردہ قواعد و طریقہ کار پر غور و خوض کرنا ۔

(v) آئین کے مقرر کردہ دیگر اختیارات کا نفاذ ۔

جنرل کونسل کا فیصلہ مندرجہ بالا معاملات کے نفاذ میں حتمی تصور ہوگا ۔

(ج) زونل بلاک اور دیگر کمیٹیوں کی کارکردگی اور اختیارات

(i) اپنی ہر ماتحت کمیٹی پر تنظیمی کنٹرول کا نفاذ ۔

(ii) ریاستی مجلس عاملہ اور جنرل کونسل کے منظور کردہ منصوبوں اور پالیسیوں کی عمل آوری اور نفاذ ۔

(iii) ان تمام فرائض کی عہدہ برآئی (عمل آوری) جو وقتاً فوقتاً ان پر عائد ہوں ۔

173

٦

(۱۵) عہدہ داروں کے فرائض اور اختیارات :۔

الف) صاحبہ صدر

ب) پارٹی کے آئین کا تحفظ

ج) ریاستی مجلس عاملہ اور جنرل کونسل کی میٹنگوں کی صدارت کرنا

نوٹ :۔ اگر میڈم چیئر پرسن کے خلاف باذریعہ پریس کی تحریک پیش کرنے کیلئے کوئی میٹنگ منعقد ہو۔ اسکی صدارت چیئر پرسن خود نہیں کرے گی۔

د) میٹنگوں میں نظم و نسق اور بہتر کارکردگی کی نگرانی۔

(۱۷) پارٹی کی کسی بھی باڈی کو طلب کرنا۔ ترتیب دینا یا ملتوی کرنا میڈم چیئر پرسن ریاستی مجلس عاملہ یا جنرل کونسل کی میٹنگ پندرہ دن کے اندر اندر طلب کرنے کی مجاز ہوگی۔ بشرطیکہ اس کا نوٹس مجلس عاملہ کے بارے میں بیس فیصد ممبروں دلنے اور جنرل کونسل کے بارے میں دس فیصد ممبروں نے دیا ہو۔

(۷) تنظیم کے فنڈس ، جائیداد اور دہ فائنانس پر کنٹرول اد سکے لئے مجلس عاملہ کا مکمل اعتماد حاصل ہو۔

(۷) تنظیم کے اندر واقع ہوجینے والی بے ضابطگیوں اور غلطیوں کا تدارک کرنا۔

(۷) اپنے کچھ اختیارات کسی زونل صدر کو اس کے زون کے حدود میں نافذ کرنے کیلئے منتقل کرنا۔

(۷) پارٹی کے آئین کے تحت دیگر تمام فرائض و اختیارات

کا نفاذ عمل آوری ۔

(۱۵) بوقت ضرورت کسی زونل بلاک یاد یگر کسی ماتحت کمیٹی کو منسوخ کرنا اور نئے انتخابات تک ُتباول انتظام کرنا ۔

(ب) نائب چیئر پرسن ۔

(ا) میڈم چیئر پرسن کی عدم موجودگی میں ان تمام فرائض و اختیارات کا نفاذ جو میڈم چیئر پرسن کو حاصل ہیں ۔

نوٹ :۔ (نائب چیئر پرسن بھی اپنے خلاف منعقدہ کسی میٹنگ کی صدارت نہیں کر سکتی)

(ج) جنرل سکریٹری :۔

(ا) جنرل سکریٹری کی تحویل میں تنظیم کی مہریں اور سا غذات ہونگے ۔ (اا) وہ تنظیم کے تمام ریکارڈ تیار کرے گی ۔

(ااا) جنرل کونسل اور سیاستی تنظیم کی میٹنگوں میں سکریٹری کے فرائض انجام دے گی ۔

نوٹ :۔(اسکے خلاف منعقدہ میٹنگ میں وہ سکریٹری کے وظائف انجام نہیں دے گی)

(۱۷) پارٹی کے آئین کے تحت تمام عائد ذمہ داریاں پوری کریگی ۔

(د) سکریٹری :۔

میڈم چیئر پرسن کے کنٹرول میں جنرل سکریٹری کے طرف سے وقتی طور پر عائد کردہ ذمہ داریوں سے عہدہ برآ ہونا ۔

(س) پبلسٹی سکریٹری :۔

(ا) پارٹی کے پروگرام اور پالیسیوں کی نشرو اشاعت ۔

(۱۱) پریس نوٹوں کی اشاعت اور پارٹی کے احکامات اور
پیدوگراموں پر مملدید آمد۔

(۱۲) میڈیم چیئر پرسن کی تاریخ منظوری ری جنرل سیکریٹری
کی عائد کردہ قیمتی ذمہ داریوں کی عمل آوری۔

(س) خزانچی :۔

(ر) تنظیم خزانچی فنڈس کا حساب رکھیگی۔

(۱۲) ریاستی مجلس عاملہ کی مقررہ کردہ آڈٹ پارٹی
کے سامنے پڑتال کیلے اپنے حسابات پیش کریگی۔

(۱۳) میڈیم چیئر پرسن کے تفویض کردہ فرائض پر عمل
پیرا ہوگی۔

(ل) نیشنل بلاک امیدواور دیگر کمیٹیوں کے عہدیداروں کے
اختیارات مندرجہ بالا عہدہ داروں کے ذمہ ہوبی فرائض
ہونگے جو ان کے بہم عہدہ مجلس عاملہ کے ہوں ماسوائے ان
اختیارات کے جو میڈیم چیئر پرسن کے حق میں آئین کی دفعہ
عشرہ کے حصہ الف کے مشتق غلا اور غلا۷ میں مذکور ہیں
(دیا ہم ایسی کمیٹیوں کی صدر اور سیکریٹریوں کے بہم عہدہ
ریاستی مجلس عاملہ کی چیئر پرسن اور جنرل سیکریٹری میں)

(حصہ چہارم)
(را انتخابات)

(۱۱) عام انتخابات :۔ تنظیم اپنے عام انتخابات برتین بیال
کے بعد ریاستی مجلس عاملہ کے مقرر کردہ مرکزی الیکشن بورڈ

کے زیرِ نگرانی عمل میں لائے گی ۔

(۱۲) انتخابات کے قواعد اور طریقِ کار :۔

پارٹی کے آئین کے دفعات کے تحت مرکزی الیکشن بورڈ
انتخابات کے قواعد اور طریقِ کار وضع کرنے اور سماجتیں
الیکشن بورڈوں کی حسب ضرورت تقرری کا مجاز ہوگا۔
مگر یہ طریقہ کار تابع منظوری ریاستی مجلسِ عاملہ ہوتگے ۔

(۱۳) کمیٹیوں اور عہدیداروں کی میعاد کا کر کرے گی :۔

تمام کمیٹیوں اور عہدیداروں کی میعاد خواہ وہ تشکیل شدہ
منتخب شدہ یا نامزد شدہ ہوں ہر حالت میں ایک عام انتخاب
سے دوسرے تمام انتخاب تک ہوگی ۔

(۱۴) مرکزی الیکشن بورڈ کی میعاد کا کر کرے گی :۔

مرکزی الیکشن بورڈ ہر عام انتخاب کے موقعہ پر تشکیل دیا
جائے گا ۔

(۱۵) ضمنی انتخاب :۔

مرکزی الیکشن بورڈ بوقت ضرورت خالی ہونے والے
عہدے کیلئے ضمنی انتخاب عمل میں لانے کا مجاز ہوگا۔

(۱۶) بانژ پریس یا شکایت کی تحریک :۔

ریاستی تنظیم یا مجلس عاملہ کے مختلف عہدیداروں کے خلاف
تحریک بانژ پریس و شکایت حسب ذیل طریقے سے پیش ہوگی ۔

۱۳

ر) میڈم چیر پرسن :۔

چیر پرسن کو اس صورت میں اپنے عہدے سے معزول
کیا جائے گا جب اسکے خلاف تحریک بازن پریس جنرل کونسل کے
ایسے دو تہائی ممبروں کی اکثریت سے پاس ہو جو رائے دہی
کے وقت موجود ہوں۔ بشرطیکہ یہ میٹنگ اسی مقصد کیلئے طلب
کی گئی ہو اور دو تہائی ممبروں کی اکثریت ہو رائے دہی کے وقت
موجود ہوں جنرل کونسل کی کل تعداد کی اکثریت میں ہوں۔ اور
چیر پرسن کو اس میٹنگ کے انعقاد سے پندرہ دن قبل مطلع کیا
گیا ہو۔ اور وائس چیر پرسن کی عدم موجودگی میں اس میٹنگ
کی صدارت ایسی خاتون کرے گی جبکہ وہ حاضرہ دے رائے دہندگان ممبرز
کی اکثریت اس مقصد کیلئے منتخب کرے اور ایسی میٹنگ جنرل کونسل
کے دس فیصد ممبروں کی نوٹس پہ جنرل سکریٹری طلب کرے گی
(ب)   وائس چیر پرسن :۔

کسی بھی وائس چیر پرسن کو ریاستی مجلس عاملہ کے حاضر اور رائے
دہندہ ممبروں کی دو تہائی اکثریت سے پاس کردہ تحریک سے ہٹایا
جائے گا۔ بشرطیکہ ان ممبروں کی تعداد ریاستی مجلس عاملہ کی کل
تعداد کی اکثریت ہو اور اسے کم از کم دس دن پہلے اس میٹنگ
کے انعقاد سے مطلع کیا گیا ہو۔

حصہ پنجم

۱۴

فنڈس

(۱۶) فنڈس بہتر کرنا :

تنظیم مندرجہ ذیل مدوں کے تحت فنڈ حاصل کر سکے گی۔

(الف) زیر رکعیت (ب) عطیہ جات (ج) چندہ

(د) تحائف (ہ) سیاسی مجلس عاملہ کا منظور کردہ دیگر طریقے۔

(۱۷) اخراجات :۔

سیاسی مجلس عاملہ اخراجات کا تعین کرے گی۔

(۱۸) آڈٹ :۔ سیاسی مجلس عاملہ کا مقرر کردہ باختیار عہدہ دار حسابات کی سالانہ پڑتال کا مجاز ہو گا۔

حصہ ششم

(متفرقات)

(۲۰) ترمیم :۔ پارٹی کے آئین یا اس کے کسی بھی حصے کی ترمیم سیاسی مجلس عاملہ کی دو تہائی ممبروں کی اکثریت سے عمل میں آئے گی۔ بشرطیکہ ترمیم کو مجلس عاملہ کے کم از کم پانچ ممبروں کے پیش کرنے پر جنرل سیکرٹری نے میٹنگ بلائی ہو۔ جنرل کونسل مجلس عاملہ کی کسی ترمیم کو منسوخ کرنے کی مجاز ہو گی۔

(۲۱) ایمرجنسی وغیرہ :۔ آئینی انتخابات ہونے تک تنظیم

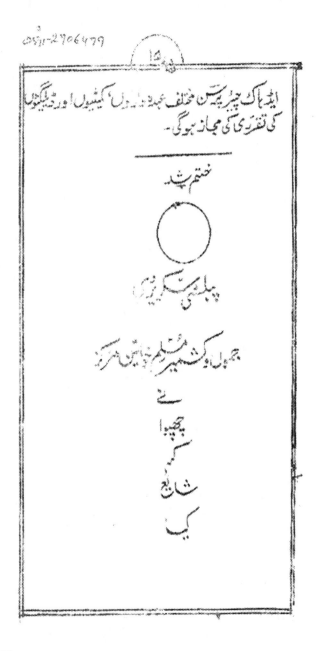

APPENDIX IV-B

CONSTITUTION OF JAMMU AND KASHMIR MUSLIM KHWATEEN-E-MARKAZ (ENGLISH TRANSLATION)

Declaration

. . . . In order to bring peace in the valley we the women of Jammu and Kashmir recognise that there is a need of consistent struggle for which we hereby declare the creation of a new party-Muslim Khwateen Markaz. The constitution of *Muslim Khwateen-e-Markaz* (herein after referred as MKM) has following postulates.

Part-1
Introduction

1. Title: It shall be called as the 'constitution of MKM'.
2. Name of the party/Organisation; Muslim Khwateen-Markaz.
3. Symbol; A flag with a sky-blue field which has a green portion and a white crescent.

4. The head-office and its area of influence: The head-office of this party shall be in Srinagar and the activities shall be carried out as per the constitutional provisions.

Part-2
Aims and Objectives:

5. MKM proposes an immediate solution to the Kashmir dispute for which it emphasises need for a dialogue through tri-party conference constituted by the members from India, Pakistan and Kashmir, which will strive to find a possible way to facilitate the use of rights of self-determination by the people of J&K, under the international charter of human Rights.

6. It shall strive for the protection of political, economical, legal, educational, cultural and religious rights of women of Jammu and Kashmir.
    a) It shall promote women artists and intellectuals.
    b) It shall recognise the problems of tribal and backward class women of valley and strive for their solution and work for their upliftement.

Part-3

7. Membership; Any woman, above 18 years of age, irrespective of caste, class or religion, who accepts the constitution and has paid all the membership fees can become a member of MKM.

8. Structure;
    a) *Muhalla yadahi* committee
    b) *Halqa* committee

c) Block Committee
d) Zonal committee
e) *Reyasati Majlise-Aamla*
f) General Council

Part-5
Funding

9. Funding sources

The organisation may generate funds in following ways;

I) Membership Fund
II) Donation
III) Charit

18. Maximum period of detention.

(1) The maximum period for which any person may be detained in pursuance of any detention order which has been confirmed under section 17, shall be—
   (a) twelve months from the date of detention in the case of persons acting in any manner prejudicial to the maintenance of public order or indulging in smuggling of timber; and
   (b) two years from the date of detention in the case of persons acting in any manner prejudicial to the security of the State.

(2) Nothing contained in this section shall affect the powers of the Government to revoke or modify the detention order at any earlier time, or extend the period of

detention of a foreigner in case his expulsion from the State has not been made possible.

20. Temporary release of persons detained.

(1) The Government may, at any time, order that a person detained in pursuance of detention order may be released for any specified period either without conditions or upon such conditions specified in the direction as that person accepts and may, at any time, cancel his release.

(2) In directing the release of any person under sub-section (1), the Government may require him to enter into a bond with or without sureties for the due observance of the conditions specified in the direction.

(3) Any person released under sub-section (1), shall surrender himself at the time and place and to the authority, specified in the order directing his release or cancelling his release as the case may be.

(4) If any person fails without sufficient cause to surrender himself in the manner specified in sub-section (3) be shall be punishable with imprisonment for a term which may extend to two years or with fine, or with both.

(5) If any person released under subsection (1) fails to fulfil any of the conditions imposed upon him under the said sub-section or in. the bond entered into by him, the bond shall be declared to be forfeited and any person bound thereby shall be liable to the penalty thereof.

(6) The period of release shall not count towards the total period of detention undergone by the person released under this section.

Source: Laws of India

http://www.lawsofindia.org/statelaw/6389/
TheJammuandKashmirPublicSafetyAct1978.html

APPENDIX III-D

MOLESTATION OF WOMEN BY STATE AGENTS THROUGH DRACONIAN ACTS:

Reported by Jammu and Kashmir Coalition of Civil Society (1990).

On may 13, 1990, Raja Ali Maradan Khan, father of Razia Sultana, R/O Booniyar Bali, Islamabad, Razia was allegedly picked up by 3rd Sikh between the Check Post and fruit forest nursery. Since that day nothing was known of his whereabouts. Razia Sultania searched for him everywhere in almost all jails throughout India. After long search, she returned to Jammu she was asked by try again in Kote Balwal Jail. Later she met several police officials and some ministers, pleading for permission to meet her father, but nothing happened. Five years later in 1995, 38 RR arrested her. They put her for five days in their custody. During these five days they tortured her and beated her ruthlessly in which she got serious head injury. After the term was over, she was realised for a brief period and then rearrested. She was tortured with electric shocks and verbal abuse. In April 2003, she was again arrested by, STF (Air Crago) Srinagar. She was ruthlessly tortured and the Inspector made her nude and beated her legs and thighs. She was released on 21 June 2003. She was again arrested and rearrested on the charges of supporting militancy. Razia however stated that she had been persuaded by different intelligence agencies in Uri for working for them, which she always refused.

Source: *State of Human Rights in Jammu and* Kashmir *1990-2005* Compiled and collated by Public Commission on Human Rights, edited by Parvez Imroz on behalf of Coalition of Civil Society, Srinagar (Delhi: Hindustan Printers, 2005)

APPENDIX III-E

THE ARMED FORCES (JAMMU AND KASHMIR) SPECIAL POWERS ACT, 1990

Excerpts

1. This Act may be called the Armed Forces (Jammu and Kashmir) Special Powers Act, 1990.
    (a) It extends to the whole of the State of Jammu and Kashmir.
    (b) It shall be deemed to have come into force on the 5th day of July, 1990.

2. Definitions. In this Act, unless the context otherwise requires,-
    (a) "armed forces" . . . .
    (b) "disturbed area" . . . .

3. Power to declare areas to be disturbed areas. If, in relation to the State of Jammu and Kashmir, the Governor of that State or the Central Government, is of opinion that the whole or any part of the State is in such a disturbed and dangerous condition that the use of armed forces in aid of the civil power is necessary to prevent—

(a) activities involving terrorist acts directed towards overawing the Government as by law established or striking terror in the people or any section of the people or alienating any section of the people or adversely affecting the harmony amongst different sections of the people;

(b) activities directed towards disclaiming, questioning or disrupting the sovereignty and territorial integrity of India or bringing about cession of a part of the territory of India or secession of a part of the territory of India front the Union or causing insult to the Indian National Flag, the Indian National Anthem and the Constitution of India, the Governor of the State or the Central Government, may, by notification in the Official Gazette, declare the whole or any part of the State to be a disturbed area.

4. Special powers of the armed forces. Any commissioned officer, warrant officer, non-commissioned officer or any other person of equivalent rank in the armed forces may, in a disturbed area,-

(a) if he is of opinion that it is necessary so to do for the maintenance of public order, after giving such due warning as he may consider necessary, fire upon or otherwise use force, even to the causing of death, against any person.

(b) if he is of opinion that it is necessary so to do, destroy any arms dump, prepared or fortified position or shelter from which armed attacks are made or are likely to be made or are attempted to be made,

(c) Arrest, without warrant, any persons who has committed a cognizable offence or against whom a reasonable suspicion exists that he has committed or is about to commit a cognizable offence and may use such force as may be necessary to effect the arrest;

(d) Enter and search, without warrant, any premises to make any such arrest as aforesaid or to recover any person believed to be wrongful restrained or confined or any property reasonably suspected to be stolen property or any arms, ammunition or explosive substances believed to be unlawful kept in such premises, and may for that purpose use such force as may be necessary, and seize any such property, arms, ammunition or explosive substances;

(e) Stop, search and seize any vehicle or vessel reasonably suspected to be carrying any person who is a proclaimed offender to commit a non-cognizable offence.

5. Power of search to include powers to break open locks, etc.

6. Arrested persons and seized property to be made over to the police. **Source:** The Gazette of India, Extraordinary, Part II-Section 1, 1990

CONCLUSION

One of the primary concerns of this work was to examine the effects of violence and armed conflict on women in Kashmir. Hopefully, this study has revealed that women have been the greatest victims of the violence in Kashmir. Looking at the major indices of development-health, education, employment and property rights-this study has shown that the militancy and armed conflict in Kashmir have had extremely destructive effects on the lives of women. The routinised cycles of violence in Kashmir have also affected the family and the household and more importantly the place of women in the families, as well. Similarly the community-kin networks have been profoundly affected by the recurring cycles of violence, and since women are the primary markers of community identities, they have been the worst affected by the disruption of community and kin ties.

The second important concern of this work was to unravel the agency of women in Kashmir. The effort was to look at women's subjectivity in the face of routinised violence to see how women shaped their lives, organised their families and maintained social ties in the wake of disruptions caused by deaths, violence and conflict.

This study has hopefully shown that women have had the most constructive engagement with the society in Kashmir. It has examined the role of women's organisations and movements in the realisation of the political goals and the fulfilment of social and cultural ideals. Indeed, this study has found ambiguities in the political roles of women's movements with some women's organisations siding with militants and the others opposing them. At the same time, women's movements in Kashmir have apparently opened up spaces of constructive dialogue and communication in the tumultuous Kashmiri society. Women's organisations have also played a crucial role in reconstructing lives and families destroyed by violence providing not only monetary support and maintenance but also emotional reassurance as well.

The present study began with a historical overview of the position of women under the Dogra rule. The first chapter of the thesis looks at the historical background and examines the impressive role of women in the independence movement. I have argued that the women in Kashmir were active political agents in the period before independence as well and fought alongside men against the oppressive rule of Dogra rule. They participated in processions, organised marches, rallies, and even took up arms against Dogra rulers. While examining the historical background, I have also examined the position of marginalised women under the Dogra rule. My study has shown that the Dogra rulers exploited the marginalised women, in particular, the prostitutes, to raise revenue for the state. Perhaps Kashmir was the only state in the pre-independence period where prostitution was both legalised and encouraged by the state. Prostitutes were registered, and the state derived considerable revenues by taxing them. The Prostitution Rules of 1921 required the prostitutes to register with the state. The Act clearly was an important instrument of state surveillance, and brought the prostitutes within the ambit of state permitting it to stake a claim over their income and resources. The independence of India in 1947 has not ruptured the deep structured alliance between the state and patriarchal forces, but has certainly substantially modified it.

The second chapter looks at the position of women in family and community life. My study has shown that the family size in Kashmir if quite modest, and the trend of large families living together is exceptionally rare in the region. Even as women are excepted to manage the household, they enjoy an 'impressive presence in the public spaces, as well. The activities of women are not confined to the domestic sphere, but include active participation, in economic and political activities, in the outside world, as well. The continual violence in Kashmir has forced parents to keep their girls away from schools, and this is reflected in the fall in literacy rate, in the post-insurgency period. My work also reveals that the health facilities for women are quite deficient, and this is reflected in the high Maternal Mortality Rate (MMR) in Kashmir. My study has revealed that about 35% of women's career choices were constrained by their families. Women's seclusion has also increased in the wake of the militant movement, but the rate of their seclusion, as it appears from my data, is higher in urban areas, and far more widespread among the upper and middle class women, as well. My study reveals that women in Kashmir are largely denied their inheritable rights in property. Only 22.5% among my respondents had received some property from their natal families. A correlation between the secessionist violence and the position of women in Kashmir is depicted by the decline in sex-ratio in post-insurgency period. My study has shown the wide prevalence of *Purdah* among women in Kashmir. While my work suggests that 73% of women observe *purdah* in Kashmir, it is only 49% among them, who actually don the *burqa*. My study reveals that the marriages are mostly arranged by the families and very few women marry according to their choice. The family system in Kashmir serves to sub-ordinate women and ensures their subjugated position in family and community life. My study also showed the prevalence of dowry, domestic violence, etc. in Kashmiri families. However I have also made an effort to unravel the routinised, everyday forms through which women challenged, resisted and negotiated the condition of their social marginalisation. Clearly the family and household were patriarchal institutions that ensured subservience of women and their subordinate position in society. The women in Kashmir, however, did manage to turn it into a resource through which they constrained the patriarchal forces to minimum disadvantage.

Chapters III and IV are concerned with the impact of violence on women's lives in Kashmir, focussing in particular, their involvement in the political domain. The study has shown that women have been the prime targets of violence in Kashmir. Women in Kashmir suffer violence not only from the external forces 'the outsiders' but also from their own kin-community members. They have been forced to don veil, and their movements have come under strict surveillance and male control. They have been forced to conform to strict dress codes and the infractions are met with severe, often violent consequences. This is because women in Kashmir are viewed as markers of cultural identity, and purity of the community rests on their chaste and refined comportment and behaviour. At the same time women have shown tremendous resilience in combating the culture of violence, organising themselves in movements and organisations through which they participate in the political process and create spaces for constructive political communication. The study has looked at the role of women in social and cultural domains and has highlighted the role of women's organisations in rebuilding lives destroyed by violence. The study has also looked at political initiatives undertaken by the women's movements. This study has noticed that there are indeed several women's movements which support the militants and their patriarchal ideologies. At the same time, these movements have not succeeded in monopolising the entire political space, and there are other movements among women who denounce them and their culture of violence. There are a large number of women's bodies which oppose violence and work to create democratic spaces in the dominant political culture in the region. Women's movements occupy an important place in the political process in Kashmir. They have been instrumental in enlarging the spaces for consensus and consent in the political process in Kashmir. More importantly, these movements have served to protect the rights of women in Kashmir and have challenged and restricted the ideologies of patriarchal domination.

BIBLIOGRAPHY

(Arranged alphabetically according to the last name)

Sources:

I. Official records

A. Government Reports/Records

Archives

National Archives of India (New Delhi), File no. 86, Foreign Department, Secret-E, March 1883

National Archives of India (New Delhi) File no. 469, Home Department, 16 November 1921

Jammu and Kashmir State Archives (Kashmir), File no. 191/h-75, Kashmir government records, Letter from Maharaja Pratab Singh to his Prime Minister, December 14 1918,

National Archives of India (New Delhi); file no. 423(2) of 1931 home/political secret, 4 September, 1931

Jammu & Kashmir Information on (issues by the bureau of Information, His Highness's Government, March 1947

National Archives of India (New Delhi) Express Letter No. 89, Political Department May, 1948

Law Reports, Rulings, etc

Jammu and Kashmir Laws Volume 18, *Private Colleges Regulation Act 2002 to Regulation Act AVT 1977* JK Law Reporter Private Ltd. New Delhi, 2005

Gazetteer, Census and Survey Reports

National Family Survey 1998-1999, *http://www.nfhsindia.org/ india2.shtml*

Census of India, J&K, 2011(Provisional), Government of India *http://censusindia.gov.in/*

Census of India, J&K, 2001(Provisional), Government of India *http://censusindia.gov.in/*

Gazetteer of India Jammu and Kashmir State, Kashmir Region Vol-1(State ed.) Bashir Ahmad, State Gazetteers Unit, Govt. Of Jammu and Kashmir, Srinagar, 1999

The Gazette of India, Extraordinary, Part II-Section 1, 1990

A. Non Government Records/Reports

State of Human Rights in Jammu and Kashmir 1990-2005 Compiled and collated by Public Commission on Human Rights, edited by Parvez Imroz on behalf of Coalition of Civil Society, Srinagar (Delhi: Hindustan Printers, 2005)

Rape and Molestation; A Weapon of War in Kashmir (A consolidated report on atrocities committed on women in Kashmir) prepared by the Jammu and Kashmir Human Rights Awareness and Documentation Centre, Srinagar, No. 32(Srinagar: Institute of Kashmir Studies, 1998)

Torture, Rape and Deaths in Custody, Report Prepared by
    Amnesty International, India; (London, 1992)
Rashid Afsana, *Waiting for Justice Widows and Half Widows*,
    Srinagar, February 2008,

I. Newspapers and Magazines
National Dailies

Indian Express
The Hindu
Guardian
Times of India
Hindustan Times

Regional Newspapers and Magazines

Greater Kashmir, English Newspaper
The Rising Kashmir, English Newspaper
The Kashmir Life, English Weekly Newspaper
Srinagar Times, Urdu Newspaper
Informative Missive, A Monthly Newsletter of Public
    Commission of Human Rights—
IZHAAR, Kashmiris Stories of Resilence, (ed.) Talib Arjumand
    Hussain and Shoba Ramachandran, Action Aid, Books for
    Change, India, 2007
Voices Unheard, A Newsletter of Kashmiri Women's Initiative for
    Peace and Disarmament-

Secondary Works

Abbott Pamella, Claire Wallace and Tyler Melissa, *An Introduction to Sociology; Feminist Perspectives,* Routledge, London, New York, (3rd edition) 2005

Abdullah Sheikh Muhammed, *Flames of the Chinar: An Autobiography,* tr. Khushwant Singh, *New York, Viking, 1993*

Ahlawat Neerja, 'Violence Against Women: Voices from the Field' in Manjit Singh and D.P Singh (Ed.), *Violence: Impact and Intervention*, Atlantic Publication, New Delhi 2008,

Alison Merinda 'Women as Agents of Political Violence: Gendering Security', *Security Dialogue,* Vol-35, 2004, p-447-463

Batalia Urvashi, *Speaking Peace, Women's Voices from Kashmir,* Kali for Women, New Delhi, 2002

Bazaz P.N. *Daughters of Vitasta; A History of Kashmiri Women From Early Times to the Present Days,* Pamposh Publications, 1959

Bhadhuri Aditi, Creating New Lives In Kashmir's Conflict Zone, *Social Welfare,* August 2009, 56(5)

Bhasin Anuradha Jamwal, Women in Kashmir Conflict: Victimhood and Beyond, IN, Shree Mulay and Jackie Kirk (ed.) *Women Building Peace Between India and Pakistan,* Anthem Press, India,

Bhasin Kamla and Ritu Menon(for India), Nighat Said Khan(for Pakistan) (ed.) *Against All Odds; Essays on Women, Religion and Development from India and Pakistan,* Kali for Women, India, 1996

Biscoe Tyndale, C.E., *Kashmir in Sunlight and Shade,* Lippincott, 1922

Browne Ken, *An Introduction to Sociology,* Polity Press, UK, 2007

Caulson N.J, *Succession in the Muslim Family,* Cambridge University Press, UK, 1971

Chenoy Anuradha and Chenoy Kamal.A.Mitra(ed.), *Maoist and Other Armed Conflict*, Penguin Books, India, 2010,

Chenoy Anuradha 'Resources or Symbols? Women and Armed Conflict in India', IN, Ava Darshan Shrestha and Rita Thapa (ed.), *The Impact of Armed Conflict on Women in South Asia*, Manohar, 2007,

Claude-Levi-Strauss, *The Elementary Structures of Kinship,* tr. James Harle Bell, John Richard von Strurner and Rodney Needham, Bostan, Beacon Press, 1969

Cooke Mariam and Angela Woolacott(ed. 1993) *Gendering War Talk,* Princeton New Jersey; Princeton University Press)

Dabla Bashir Ahmad, *A Sociological Study of Widows and Orphans in Kashmir,* JAYKAY Publications, Srinagar, 2010

Dabla Bashir Ahmad, *Domestic Violence Against Women In Kashmir Valley,* JAYKAY Publications, Srinagar, 2009

Dabla Bashir Ahmad, *Multi-dimensional Problems of Women in Kashmir*, Gyan Publications, India, 2007

Dabla Bashir Ahmad, Sandeep.K.Nayak, Khurshid—ul-Islam(ed.), *Gender Discrimination In the Kashmir Valley; A Survey of Budgam and Baramulla Districts,* Gyan Publications, Delhi, 2000

Dabla, Bashir Ahmad *Sociological Papers on Kashmir, Volume 1 and 2,* JAYKAY publications, Srinagar, 2010

Darshan Ava Shrestha and Rita Thapa (ed.), *The Impact of Armed Conflict on Women in South Asia,* Manohar Publications, 2007

Dasgupta Jyoti Bhusan, *Jammu and Kashmir,* The Hague: Martinus Nijhoff, *1968*

Devi Radha, *Timing of Marriage in India, Vision and Reality,* IN, Kamal K. Misra, Janet Huber Lowry,(ed.), *Recent Studies on Indian Women Empirical Work of Social Scientists,* Rawat publications, 2007

Dewan Ritu, 'Humsheera', 'Humsaya': Sisters, Neighbours, Women's Testimonies from Kashmir, *Economic and Political Weekly,* Oct-8 1994, p—2655

Dost Muhammed and Bhat A.S., *Family in Kashmir,* IN, (ed.) Gulshan Majeed, *Look n Kashmir from Ancient and Modern,* Jay Kay Books, Srinagar, 2006

Dube Leela, *Women and Kinship, Comparative Perspectives on Gender in South and South East Asia,* Rawat publications, India 2009

Farooq Fayaz, *Folklore and History of Kashmir,* Nunaposh Publications Srinagar, 2002,

Fyzee, A.A, *Outlines of Muhammadan Law,* Fourth Edition, New Delhi 1999

Ghosh Sobha Venkatesh, *Contextualizing Domestic Violence: Family Community, State,* IN, Rinki Bhattacharya, *Behind Closed Doors, Domestic Violence in India,* Sage Publications, New Delhi

Goode, J.William, World Revolutions and Family Patterns, Collier Macmillan, New York 1963

Habib Anjum Zamruda, *Prisoner No.100, My Life In An Indian Prison,* tr. Sahiba Hussain, Zubaan, New Delhi,2011

Hasan Mushirul, *Nationalism and Communal Politics in India, 1855-1930,* Manohar Publications 1991

Hassnain F.M. (ed.), *Kashmir Misgovernment,* Robert Thorp, Gulshan Publications, Srinagar, Kashmir, India, second edition 2011

Ibrahim Francis, *Contemporary Sociology; An Introduction To Concepts and Theories,* Oxford University Press, New Delhi 2006

Kashani Sarwan, Idrees Kanth and Gowhar Fazili, *The Impact of Violence on the Student Community in Kashmir*, Delhi, Oxford India Trust, 2003

Kaw M.K, *Kashmir and its People Studies in the Evolution of Kashmiri Society*, APH publishing corporation, New Delhi, India, 2004

Kazi Seema, *Between Democracy and Nation-Gender and Militarization in Kashmir*, Women Unlimited, New Delhi, 2009

Khajooria Bhawana, 'Political Roles of Women in Kashmir' IN, Malashri Lal, Sukrita Paul Kumar (ed.) *Women's Studies in India, Contours of Change*, Indian Institute of Advanced Study, Shimla 2002

Khan G.H, *Freedom Movement in Kashmir 1931-1940*; Light and Life Publications, New Delhi, Jammu, Trivandrum, 1980

Khan Mohammed Ishaq, *History of Srinagar 1846-1947, A Study in Socio-Cultural Change*, Gulshan Publications, Srinagar, second edition, 1999

Khan Nyla Ali, *Islam, Women and Violence in Kashmir; Between India and Pakistan*, Palgrave Macmillan, New York, 2010

Kumkum Sangari, Marking time: The Gendered Present and the Nuclear Future, IN, *Nivedini Journal of Gender Studies*, Volume 13, October November 2007,

Maithre Wickramasinghe, *Feminist Research Methodology-Making Meanings of Meaning Making*, Routledge, USA, 2010,

Manchanda Rita (ed.), *Women, War and Peace in South Asia; Beyond Victimhood to Agency*, Sage Publications, New Delhi, 2001

Manchanda Rita, 'Women's Agency in Peace building; Gender Relations in Post-Conflict Construction, *Economic and Political Weekly*, Vol.40, No.44/45, (Oct 29-Nov 4) 2005,

Manchanda Rita, Women's Agency in Peace Building: Gender Relations in Post-Conflict Construction, EPW, Vol. 40, No.44/45, (Oct 29-Nov 4) 2005,

Maqbool Sahil, 'Tehreke-Mazahamat Mein Khuwatein ka Role—1', IN, *Tanazaaye Kashmir, Tarikh Ke Aainey Me,* Vol 1

Matoo Suhaib, Profiling a Crusader, *Greater Kashmir,* 18 August 2009

Menon Ritu and Kamla Bhasin, *Borders and Boundaries: Women in India's Partition.* New Delhi: Kali for Women, 1998.

Merry Sally Engle, *Gender Violence; A Cultural Perspective, Introductions to Engaged Anthropology,* Wiley-Blackwell, 2009

Minault Gail, *The Khilafat Movement: Religious Symbolism and Mobilization,* Columbia University Press, India, 1982

Mishra Saraswati, *Status of Indian Women,* Gyan Publishing House, New Delhi 2002 pp-114

Mohsin Amena, Silence and Marginality: Gendered Security and The Nation State, IN, Fazal Farah, Rajagopalan Swarna(ed.) *Women Security and South Asia-A Clearing for the Thicket,* Sage Publication, New Delhi, 2005

Morgan D, 'Risk and Family Practices', IN, E. Silva and C. Smart (eds.), *The New Family,* London Sage, 1999

Oakley.A, Interviewing Women: A Contradiction in Terms, IN Roberts, H. (ed.). *Doing Feminist Research,* London: Routledge & Kegan Paul, 1981

Parahar Swati, 'Gender Jihad Jingoism; Women as Perpetrators, Planners and Patrons of Militancy in Kashmir', *Studies in Conflict Terrorism,* Volume: 34, Issue: 4, TAYLOR & FRANCIS, 2011

Parashar Swati, Feminist IR and Women Militants: Case Studies from South Asia" IN Cambridge Review of International Affairs, June 2009

Qayoom Shabnum, *Kashmir Me Khwateen be-Hurmati,* Waqar Publications, Srinagar, edition 4, 2010,

Rai Usha, The Healing Touch of Rahat Ghar, *The Hindu,* 08-oct-2006

Rajagopalan Swarna, 'Women and Security: In Search of a New Paradigm' IN Faizal Sarah and Swarna,(ed;)

Ramachandran Sudha, *The Shades of Violence; Women and Kashmir,* WISCOMP, New Delhi 2003

Saliba Therese, Carolyn Allen, and Judith A. Howard, *Gender, Politics and Islam,* Orient Longman Private Limited, New Delhi, India, 2005

Sangh Mittra and Bachan Kumar, *Encyclopedia of Women in South Asia,* Vol.1, Kalpaz Publications, Delhi, 2004

Saraf Mohammed Yusuf, *Kashmiri's Fight—For Freedom* Vol.1 (1819-1946), Ferozons ltd, Lahore, Pakistan, 1977

Shafi Aneesa, *Working Women In Kashmir, Problems and Prospects,* APH Publications, Delhi, 2002

Shah A.M, 'Basic Terms and Concepts in the Study of the Family in India', *Indian Economic and Social History Review,* Sage Publication, Vol 1 No.3, January-March, 1964

Sharma Urrula, *Dowry in North India; Its Consequences For Women,* IN, R.Hirschon (ed.) Women and Poverty; Women as Property, London Croon Helm, 1984

Social, Economic and Educational Status of the Muslim Community of India, A Report, Prime Minister's High Level Committee Cabinet Secretariat Government of India November, 2006

Suri Kavita, *Impact of Violence on Women's Education in Kashmir,* WISCOMP, New Delhi, 2006

Tasir Rashid, *Tarikh-e-Hurriyat-i-Kashmir,* Srinagar, Muhaffiz publication 1968

Tremblay Reeta Chowdhari, *Identity and Nationalism: Where are Women in Kashmiri politics?* IN, Shree Mulay and Jakie Kirk (ed.)

Visaria Leela, 'Violence Against Women in India: Is Empowerment a Protective Factor?' *Economic and Political Weekly,* Nov 29 2008.

Walikhanna Charu, *Women Silent Victims In Armed Conflict; An Area Study Of Jammu And Kashmir,* Serial Publications, 2004,

Wani Afzal, *Kashmir University Law Review,* 1996

Women's Feature Service and Sangat, Fearless Nighat, *Social Welfare,* September 2007, 54(6),

Yasin Madhvi, 'Role of Women in Freedom Struggle of Kashmir', IN Mohammed Yasin and Qayum Yasin(ed.) *History of the Freedom Struggle in Jammu & Kashmir,* Light and Life Publishers, New Delhi,

Yasin Mohammed, Madhavi Yasin(ed.), *Mysteries and Glimpses of Kashmir,* Raj Publications, New Delhi, 1996,

Websites:

Official website, Guild of Service
www.guildofservice.org/projects.php#raahatghar
Official Website of Jammu and Kashmir Women's Development corporation
www.JKWDC.com,
A news website from Kashmir containing conflict data *www. kmsnew.org*
Uppsala University, Conflict data program available at *http:// www.pcr.uu.se/research/UCDP/links-faq/faq.htm*
Independent Women's Initiative for Justice, Shopian Case Watch 2009 *http://kafilabackup.files.wordpress.com/2009/12/*

iwij-report-shopian-10-dec-2009.pdf, retrieved from *www. Kashmirtimes.com*

Jaleel Muzammil, Spawning Militancy: The Rise of Hizbul, 22 May 2003, *The Indian Express http://www.jammuKashmir. com/archives/archives2003/Kashmir20030522d.html*

Rape In Kashmir. A Crime of War, *Asia Watch, A Division of Human Rights Watch & Physicians for Human Rights http:// www.hrw.org/sites/default/files/reports/INDIA935.PDF*

Siddiqui Saeed-ur-Rehman, 'Women day in Kashmir' *Wailing Woes, http://www.Kashmirnewz.com/a0027.html*

Domestic Violence *http://www.measuredhs.com/pubs/pdf/ FRIND3/15Chapter15.pdf*

Gender Disparity And Policies Of Inclusion: A Case study of Women's Education In Jammu and Kashmir *http://www. researchersworld.com/vol2/issue3/Paper_16.pdf*

Goswami Roshni, *Reinforcing Subordination, An Analysis of Women in Armed Conflict Situations*

www.isiswomen.org /wia/wia399/ pea00001.html

Hajam Mohammed Subhan, A Barber's Revolution, *http:// jkalternativeviewpoint.com/statenews.php?link=5752*

Half Widow-Half life, Responding to Gendered Violence in Kashmir, A report by Association of Parents of Disappeared persons, *http://kafilabackup.files.wordpress.com/2011/07/half-widow-half-wife-apdp-report.pdf*

Haque M.Mazharul, 'Profile: Asiya Andrabi: Warrior in Veil,' *The Milii Gazette* 3(17) (1-15 September 2002).

www.miligazette. com/archives/01092002/0109200264.html

Militant In Her: Women and Resistance

http://english.Aljazeeranet/indepth/spotlight/ Kashmirtheforgottenconflict/2011/07/201173/9958721770. html.

Prevention of Immoral Trafficking Prevention Act,1956

http://ncpcr.gov.in/Acts/Immoral_Traffic_Prevention_Act_(ITPA)_1956.pdf

Anti-domestic violence bill introduced in Kashmir assembly
http://sify.com/news/anti-domestic-violence-bill-introduced-in-Kashmir-assembly-news-national-kd0u4ceihga.html

Jammu and Kashmir women's commission chief bats for introduction of Women's Reservation Bill
http://www.dnaindia. com/india/report_ jammu-and-Kashmir-women-s-commission-chief-bats-for-introduction-of-women-s-reservation-bill_1367299

Official Website of District Anantnag, Government of J&K
http://anantnag.nic.in/

Official Website of District Srinagar,
http://srinagar.nic.in/districtprofile/districtprofile.htm,

Report on Education Sector in Jammu and Kashmir State, by Jammu & Kashmir Institute of Management, Public Administration & Rural Development *http://cbpr.yashada.org/content/jammu_and_Kashmir/education_sector_report.pdf*